Three Rivers Crossed

Copyright © 2011 Linda Jean Hall

All rights reserved. ©Nneka Publications.

Third Printing: 2012

Editor: Savannah Blanchard

ISBN: 146356922X

ISBN-13: 978-1463569228

DEDICATION

¡A mis familias en todas partes del mundo
Y a la nueva vida
Para todos!

A Linda Fardan, a Curtis Edward Fairfax,
a mis amores los que están en el cielo....
Y a ti, m'ito menor....gracias por el título!

Real parents are the ones that love you.....

"Mom and Dad"

James Washington
(1900-1964)

Hallie White Washington
(1903-1963)

Map of the Village in Ross Township, PA

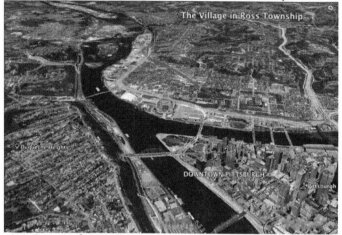

Map Courtesy of: © Google 2012, Image © Terrametrics 2012, Image NOAA.

FOREWORD

Three Rivers Crossed is a marvelous, engaging and spirited story of the coming of age of a remarkable young woman in Pittsburgh. Many books chronicle the lives of the rich and famous, but Linda Hall's life story resonates precisely because it speaks to the great majority of us, who are neither rich nor famous nor notorious. Were they written, our lives also would tell fascinating stories of struggle and the will to succeed. For that reason, many of us will look to Linda's story and nod our heads knowingly for the universal truths it contains about ourselves. I will be using *Three Rivers Crossed* in my course on the History of Black Pittsburgh; my students are in for a treat. –

>Laurence Glasco, *Associate Professor of History, University of Pittsburgh*

ACKNOWLEDGEMENTS

Illustrators
Holly N. Avery
Deanna Graves

*

Department of Art,
University of California at Santa Barbara

*

Cover Design
Peter Allen

*

Graphic and Content Design
Micah E. Hall

Introduction

In a small town, close to where the Monongahela and Allegheny Rivers feed the Ohio River, the life of one individual began without much anticipation. *Three Rivers Crossed* reveals how fundamental life skills are acquired, and countless steps are taken by a child who lived in the northern rolling hills of the three rivers during the post-World War II era between 1948 and 1966. The memoir is a come to maturity tale of a search by an Afro-American female as she begins a very arduous journey along the pathway to an unsure future.

The story begins in Pittsburgh's North side district, to explain how and why the child was destined to repeatedly transverse the streams. Many events take place in the Borough of Bellevue, and in Ross Township within an isolated community referred to as the "Village." Family ties in the Village are strong and the child is swept up and nurtured by the many extended families whose names include: Washington, Thompson, Brown, Brogdon, Carter, Clinton, Burton, Parker, Robinson, Piper, Kelly, McRoberts, and Crenshaw. The Village is not a recognized and celebrated black community like its culturally distinct next door neighbors of Manchester and the North Side, or the upper and lower Hill District across town. *Three Rivers Crossed* unapologetically provides a humorous insight into two of the most sacred of institutions of the Black community, the church and the family. The memoir is frank, honest, and it painfully dissects the child's development in simple language that rings true for current generations. This book is inspired by and dedicated to the loving memories of the many aunties who nurtured the child in the Village: Clare Clinton, Felda Thompson, Florence Brogdon, and Louise Robinson, and her parents of the heart, James and Hallie Washington.

Many events in the book are of great historical significance because they are marks denoting social metamorphoses in American society. Little known opinions about these events, that ran through the Black community, are included to demonstrate how these helped to shape the child and prepare her to leave the Village. The memoir confronts critical topics such as, traumatic death, war, national changes in discriminatory practices and the tumultuous impact to families during the financial booms and busts of the time span within the text. The Village prepared the child in its particular way to participate in the changes that rocked America's personal identity.

Three Rivers Crossed was initially written to exorcise the tortured soul of the woman who was the child in the Village. The novel is an emotional tribute to the residents of a now lost and small black community at the fringes of North Hills. Several initial readers who are lifelong educators recognized the book's relevance as a teaching tool in the areas of History, Black Studies and Feminine Studies. The initial release was well received and enthusiastically supported towards its current and more mature edition by Professor Laurance Glasco, noted Historian and educator at the University of Pittsburgh. During the Christmas holiday in 2011, the author sat in the Porch restaurant with Professor Glasco directly in front of the Cathedral of Learning on Pitt's campus to discuss her life and the work. The symbolism of this event was poignant because during her formative years, the author frequently walked from the North Side to the Cathedral to sit for hours in the Commons where she always felt connected to her destiny and at peace. The final touches to prepare this work for formal publication – a book that would tell her story -- would be compiled based on the insight and contributions of Professor Glasco in the shadow of the same edifice in which she was inspired to create a future.

L. J. H.

Three Rivers Crossed

Linda Jean Hall

CHAPTER 1 -- THE RESCUE

The chestnut brown-skinned, attractive woman was pregnant again. This was not a happy event and she wasn't making any effort to hide her disappointment. The brutally hot late July weather in a sweltering inner city without shelter left her absolutely nowhere to hide to collect her thoughts. Despite possessing an abundance of pride, she and her common-law husband shared a life that consisted of stumbling from relative to relative with their two existing children in tow.

Her requests for temporary shelter were always emotional and pitiful. In most cases, without any notice, she would suddenly appear on a relative's doorstep. She dressed the children in clean but tattered clothing. There was also no attempt on her part to mask the obvious sadness in their eyes. They were only ages one and two and both were unusually well behaved.

She slowly and tearfully would begin a well-practiced appeal for assistance. This always included the promise of only a short term stay. If there seemed to be any doubt regarding the behavior of her children she would add, "Oh, don't worry about them. They're very quiet. They'll be good." She was extremely convincing.

There was absolutely no doubt that there was a need to help. The family members were usually very touched and gladly responded by reaching out to protect their sibling. Their generosity was based on a shared religious upbringing and a commitment they all had made to their parents to help any member of the family to grab a piece of the American Dream. All twelve of her brothers and sisters fought hard to forget that even as a child she had been obstinate and a bit strange. They couldn't deny her basic shelter as she stood before them undeniably pregnant, desperately clinging to the hand of her young son and protectively carrying the eldest child on her hip.

Unfortunately, soon after she and the children were given shelter, the small and thin common-law husband always appeared. He did not interact with his generous hosts in anyway. They found him at first to be cordial and their sister's commitment to him almost cult-like. She more than loved what appeared to her relatives to be a feeble man who was a bit too content to be an usher at a downtown theatre. His control over her was silent. Within a short period of time, his presence in the home became downright unsettling.

The situation rapidly deteriorated. The family discovered that the common-law husband was the subject of a vicious rumor. According to what was felt to be reliable information, he was suspected of having a legitimate wife and two other children. This possibility did not have to be confirmed. In those days, a man was judged strictly on his reputation. His aloofness was deemed to be a sign that he was ungrateful and the chatter about his other family only made his presence more irritating.

She could not or would not recognize that her situation was sad and headed for a possible horrible conclusion. Perhaps this was due to her desperate fight to protect the growing number of secrets about her relationships. Her strong will and often pretentious nature always seemed to get in the way. Earnest attempts by her siblings to simply talk to her usually turned into shoving and shouting matches. Together and without much effort, she and her mate consistently wore out their welcome.

There had been no indication that she would inherit what appeared to be a self-destructive nature. Her father migrated to Pittsburgh from North Carolina. He was proud of the fact that he had been able to acquire property and prestige even during the Great Depression. His wife's dazzling American-Indian and Black heritage combined to make her a striking beauty. They generously welcomed visitors to their warm home for countless dinners and treated their guests like members of the family. The couple was viewed as a pillar of the mid-city church where he was a deacon and a member of a renowned mass choir.

During the long marriage of her parents, thirteen children had been born. Even their enemies had to admit that they were all in some way exceptionally intelligent and attractive. Most had attained some form of success and stability in their lives. Those with their own families found it difficult to emotionally support their now twenty-five year old unmarried sister who proudly carried the third child of a man they barely knew.

The growing rumor about the common-law husband's supposed infidelity continued to circulate freely. One family member even added fuel to the fire by saying that he'd seen one of the children of the suspected marriage. He added that the child looked suspiciously like the older child of their sister's union. The common-law husband's only salvation was his personal appearance. He was half white and had a mass of beautiful wavy black hair. These characteristics were greatly envied at this time in the history of Black America. But his looks did not save him from eviction. Often, he appeared at family dinners to be overly tired and weak despite the fact that he was only in his mid-twenties. At some point it was confirmed that he had a congenital heart condition.

The couple and their children were disruptive guests in the homes of her siblings. Numerous problems came about simply because of their attitudes. They never could seem to reach a point were they were able to be self-sufficient. Their presence drained resources slowly from the pockets of their benefactors. Eventually, it always became blatantly obvious that without a strong push out the door, they would never voluntarily leave.

They once again found themselves without permanent housing on the eve of the birth of the new arrival. A close friend agreed to let them move in. She also volunteered to keep an eye on the children as the young mother left for the hospital to bring another baby into the world. The future was not promising. This birth would bring another mouth to feed into their care for which they could not provide even a roof to put over its head. They were a couple that seemed to be playing at being parents.

The labor was uneventful and the baby was of average height and weight. Shortly after the birth, the child was presented to her father. He uttered only a few words of bitter welcome to his daughter. "I don't want another damn split tailed girl." He repeated this phrase over and over to anyone who would listen. In horror, the hospital staff noted his rejection. They all wondered what would become of this unwanted child.

The baby was full-term, healthy and it strongly resembled its older sister and brother. Everyone hoped that before the end of the required four day hospital stay that the father would overcome his obvious strong dislike of the child. However, with each passing day his unrighteous indignation only intensified. One nurse expressed deep concern for the well-being of the baby to the attending physician. The doctor dismissed her comments by assuring her that he was sure the father's rejection was only temporary. The father continued to deny the child and his harsh statements and overall disgust did not in any way decrease.

The situation was only to grow more confusing. Within only a week of the delivery, in August of 1948, the mother abruptly broke all ties with her siblings. They were disappointed, but secretly cherished the peace and quiet that replaced their sister's unexpected disruptions into their personal lives. By now, they were worn raw by her frequent visits and the unending turmoil that surrounded her tumultuous lifestyle.

The baby was given into the care of a friend of the family. The reason for this decision was to become yet another protected secret. The mother's siblings never had an opportunity to even see their new niece and were only left to wonder what had happened to totally alienate their sister. It was at this point that the young mother, father and other two children abruptly left Pittsburgh and moved into a condominium in Cleveland, Ohio. No arrangements were made to ever retrieve the missing member of their illegitimate family.

The baby remained in Pittsburgh in the hands of a reluctant personal friend of the mother. There, for the most part, it was left to lay in its own feces and urine. The meager supply of clean diapers left by its mother had only lasted a few days. Its crib was little more than a cardboard box that sat diagonally in a dark, humid corner of a small room.

The only time the apartment was cool was in the late evening. Even then, the room remained unbearably hot. Soon the roaches found their way into the baby's diaper. The friend was unwilling or unable to purchase food to feed the infant. It was perhaps for this reason she soon sought help from a cousin of the baby's grandfather who lived several miles outside the city.

The infant was almost a month old by the time the reluctant caretaker finally approached the family for help. The cousin agreed to drop by and she expected to find a happy cooing infant. She brought along a few dollars cash because she planned to leave the funds with the caretaker to help buy food and maybe even a new outfit for the baby. Instead, she was horrified to see a child that was on the verge of dying. The baby appeared to be less than four pounds in weight and she lay motionless in the filthy makeshift crib. Despite the efforts of the caretaker to wake the baby, it remained unresponsive. It was obvious that it didn't even have the strength to cry.

Outrage and horror filled the cousin's heart. Tears began to roll down her face as she reached into the crib to touch the soft and pale skin of the infant.

The caretaker lit a cigarette and while standing over the baby she proclaimed her innocence and said, "I just want it out of here. It's sick or something. It won't eat a damn thing. I told her mother I would only watch her for so long. Shit, I don't even know what its name is. I've had enough and it sure ain't gonna lie up in here and die on me."

The cousin was now almost beside herself with anger. She purposefully took a step back in an effort to control her temper. The temptation to slap the hateful caretaker did occur to her, but she resisted. This was not the time to deal with her. Without hesitation and another word, she pushed the woman aside and scooped the infant from the soiled blankets. With the baby held close to her, she now realized it was barely breathing and extremely hot and clammy. She turned to face the caretaker and demanded something clean to cover the infant. The emaciated baby was then carefully wrapped in a dingy sheet.

The cousin's reputation had preceded her. The caretaker realized that it was not uncommon for this woman to confront even men one on one. She knew that it would be unwise to antagonize her. Therefore, she quickly began to backup towards the doorway of the room. The cousin glared at her and said, "Where the hell are you going? Call me a cab! Now!"

The taxi arrived within a few minutes because the cab stand was only a few miles from the apartment. The caretaker was now too terrified to move without permission. She made a vain attempt to gather the cousin's purse as she prepared to leave. This effort was aborted when the cousin in a voice that could cut ice instructed her, "Don't touch my shit. The cabdriver will get it."

Within the hour, the cousin managed to have the baby seen by her family physician. She was informed that within another few hours the child might have died. The doctor also warned her that she should not grow too attached to the baby. There was still a strong possibility that it would still not survive. His sobering words did not deter her from accepting the responsibility.

Her determination extended into hours and days in which she gently and almost constantly held the weak infant. She prayed, rocked, and sung to the child while feeding it the doctor's rich prescribed formula based on Carnation Evaporated Milk. At first, the baby could only tolerate a few meager sips. She remained committed and determined as the intake level gradually increased. It was possibly at this time that in her heart she became the true mother of the unwanted infant.

When the child was strong enough she was relieved to welcome it into her home and into her community.

"I just want it out of here. It's sick or something." Illustrated by Deanna Graves 2012.

CHAPTER 2 -- THE COMMUNITY

The previous story of the unwanted baby is a compilation of accounts of what I've been told were my humble beginnings. It is based on the sometimes murky contributions of various relatives and friends over the years. Whatever the truth of this story might be, it was with this package of rejection and confusion that I entered the Village. At that time, the Village was a collection of twenty or more modest row houses. It was a secluded black community completely encircled by a Caucasian neighborhood.

I began to develop my own memories around the same time that I started to attend school. This was during the mid 50's. I vividly recall that I always cherished the long walks from school or visits to the grocery store. Everything of importance like school and any store were all outside the boundaries of the Village. These peaceful and slow excursions included glimpses of the magnificent houses with manicured lawns, sparkling windows and fancy potted plants of the surrounding neighborhood. I always found it comforting that the non-indigenous and beautiful seasonal indicators were taken inside to provide them shelter from the cold winter months. Miraculously, they would reappear and remain proudly displayed outside during the short Pennsylvania late spring and summer.

After school the big yellow bus bounced and rattled, stopping every so often to deposit some of its contents here and there. It was a safe time for children of any color to walk to and from school. In fact, during the long summer evenings we usually played "hide-and-go-seek" almost until it was time to go to bed. Seasoned players hid safely beneath a neighbor's porch or beside a garage in the alley that cut through the center of our Village. The only "bogeyman" was imaginary. He was utilized to keep you in your place as a child. Without a doubt, we knew our place. Almost everyday we were not so gently reminded that our place was to be, "seen and not heard."

Parents were proficient at hollering from their porches to summon the children. Each child knew the sound of his parent's voice. We would try to tear ourselves away from whatever game we happened to be playing in order to provide a prompt response. Our shouts were breathless, curt and usually uttered while running towards our homes. It was especially important to avoid hearing a second summons or whistle. These were immediately accompanied by a direct indication of what would happen if you had to be called a third time.

The neighborhood that surrounded the racially exclusive and isolated Village was pristine. It had elevated sidewalks with discreetly placed gutters. This drainage system and anything that would disturb the propriety of the area was hidden from view. The sidewalks were incredibly broad from my perspective. We adhered to the golden rule governing childhood as we strolled along these streets: "step on a crack and you'll break your mother's back." As we walked, we tried to relax and avoid looking silly as we purposefully took baby or oversized steps to avoid anything that looked like a break in the pavement.

This environment inspired the creation of games played with sticks, leaves and stones found along the way. Huge oak and maple trees were shelter from the wind, snow and rain. Large piles of multi-colored, warm autumn leaves became fleets of conquering vessels as they were washed by the chilly and gentle fall rains into the grates of the hidden gutters.

The bus driver, crossing guard, teachers, principal, cafeteria workers and the vast majority of people who taught or provided services for the school system were not Hispanic, not Asian, or Black. On the way home the bus stop for the colored children was the last stop but we were never the first to be picked up in the morning. The reality of this was that we usually had to stand up the entire four mile ride to school.

We were a small group of children of color that spent our weekdays with one foot in a white world of straight or naturally curly blond, brunette and red hair. Our parents were employed to keep the neighborhood households clean and the lawns cut. Each day our mothers packed lunches for us and our white peers in the neighborhood. Even with this in common it did not seem to increase the comfort level at school of either group of children.

We were not aware of what our white fellow students did after school. In most cases, we did not know what their parents looked like or what they did for a living. What we did know was that the homes of our white classmates were larger, cleaner, and newer and every one of them had running water and inside toilets. The public works department did not extend water services to all the homes in the small Village.

Existence within the Village defied logic and our lives lacked social justice. It was a time in which the chips were held by the majority and the minority barely mattered. It didn't take me or my black and white peers long to figure out what our real places were in this society.

Some homes in the Village were well-kept. The one to which the cousin brought me was not. The house was outside the utility parameter and therefore one of those not qualified to receive water services. This translated to mean there was a need for a horrid outside toilet and no running water – cold or hot. A small spring supplied water for all household needs. The trick was to try to keep a supply of fresh water inside the house. This basic need resulted in the creation of a twice-a-day chore that usually required at least two hours to complete. I repeatedly dipped buckets in the spring and carried these to large boiling kettles on top of the stove. At the end of everyday it was my responsibility to dispose of the dirty water after bathing or washing clothes.

We had an outside toilet that was an unpainted shed. It sat at the far corner of the property, downwind from the house. My father cared for this facility. He'd frequently face the horde of flies at the rear of the building in order to spread lime or redistribute the contents. We also had what we called a slop jar. This white, pot-shaped device was used mostly at night as our indoor toilet. As I grew older, it became my job to empty this behind the outside toilet.

The house was seated at the foot of a gully, close to the banks of a creek whose source was never found. The yard was naturally home to all sorts of useless vegetation. Frightening and sometimes dangerous snakes and other creatures were never far from our door. A meticulous old-fashioned liberty garden of potatoes, corn and greens was used to supplement the sparse diet that too often centered on meat stables such as neck bones, chicken backs and wings.

There was always a task undone and the work increased in volume as the house continued to fall more and more into disrepair. I became aware that inside our creaking home there existed a relentless form of poverty. At some point, I started to feel sorry for myself. I developed a hatred for the humbling work that never ended. I would have done anything to escape.

CHAPTER 3 – BABY-BABY AND THE VILLAGE

My entire life I've never been certain that the name I use every day is really my name. At the end of the first month in the care of my new family, their daughter gave me the simple nickname, Baby-Baby. The distant cousins, who were now my acting mother and father, refused to use the generic nickname. They said that it only increased their sadness about the whole thing to even hear it. Soon my cousin-mother ventured to the hospital where I was born. Somehow, she was able to acquire a copy of an official birth certificate. It indicated that my name was actually Jean. She hid the document in a trunk. At her insistence, from that point forward I was to use her last name. The entire Village understood that this meant that I also received the blessing of her protection from the cruel parents that had abandoned me.

According to the legend, I quickly overcame the near-death experience without any after effects. My status with the distant cousins was to always be "nearly adopted." I was never officially granted the legal benefit of their name. The kindhearted new parents didn't dare approach the courts to start adoption proceedings. They felt that there was a slight possibility that the real mother might try to reassert her parental rights. The reason I was given for this possibility was that my real mother was a prideful woman who frequently made very bad decisions.

The aging couple was one of the founding members of the Village. Therefore they were held in high regard as such by the Village and the neighborhood. After much personal sacrifice during the Great Depression, they managed to send a daughter, their only child, to college at Tuskegee Institute. Unfortunately, the daughter soon developed an excessive appetite for alcohol and despicable men. She seemed to find it easy to abandon the hopes of her parents whenever she had too much to drink. The times she was intoxicated far outnumbered the times she was sober.

During my early years in school, my parents were energetic, active and supportive. The bad experience of raising their daughter didn't seem to taint their relationship with me. Even though my arrival came late in their lives, they generously and consistently provided me with love and understanding.

During this time, I did not focus on my growing resentment. I accepted the stench of the slop jar and unending trips to the spring without protest. I just wanted to be a "good girl" in the eyes of my new family. Unfortunately, the desire to find what I considered a better life continued to grow inside my heart. I started to take the nurturing environment for granted.

One means of escape from the cluttered house beside the creek could be accomplished almost daily by making a trip to the grocery store. It and all the other types of stores were located outside the Village. These peaceful excursions provided me with the hope that I would someday be able to enter those beautiful homes of the neighborhood and sit on their comfortable sofas. I just knew somehow that I could belong to the world that existed beyond the glass and wooden doors. The emotion I harbored was not envy. I sincerely wanted to find a clean and orderly way of living. Somewhere, I felt there must be a place where even a person without a real name of their own could be accepted.

For almost seven years, I kept this ungrateful and immature longing hidden. Even when I was very young, I realized that it was not wise to say everything you were thinking. I kept my delegated place as a child. This was done out of respect for my elders as much as a lack of interest in sharing my feelings with my new parents. It was as if I had a family, but I really didn't. I was a part of something, but I really wasn't a part of anything. As my feelings of insecurity grew, so did the rift between me and my new family.

The Village was not a place that harbored secrets. Most things done in the dark made their way to common knowledge. However, there was one thing that was never explained or even discussed. Long ago, a very tall and thick hedge had been planted to divide the only street that went directly from their neighborhood to our Village. This absolutely prevented us from driving or walking amongst the homes of our closest white neighbors. Beneath the hedge ran a shallow gutter and behind it a chain link fence. We, as children of the Village, did not know who planted the hedge. The adults never discussed the hedge in front of the children. Asking the adults about any small matter was out of the question. Therefore, none of us asked our parents to explain the hedge, even after we became young adults.

The Village had been founded almost by accident. It was situated on property that was once part of a path between two sections of the surrounding Caucasian neighborhood. The houses had been built by the new arrivals from the south during the great migration of blacks in the late '30s and '40s. These simple frame houses were the first property ever acquired by most of the Village members. Some of our elders could trace their roots only one generation back to some form of slavery in Virginia or the Carolinas. The strong southern roots of the Village assured that our parents would at least try to instill in us a faith in education and a positive attitude about our place in the future.

CHAPTER 4 -- FAMILIES AND PLAY COUSINS

The majority of the families in the Village were related in some way. There was definitely strength in numbers. Some members of our generation tried to dominate the rest of us by threatening or delivering severe intimidation or undeserved physical punishment. This created an unstable situation for the few of us in the Village that had small family units. After all, even a bully has a limit to the number of people he can fight at one time.

I tried to establish alliances with my friends who had larger families. This strategy worked only some of the time. I never knew when the parents of one of my friends would decide to move. When this happened, it was possible that the entire social structure would also change with their departure. The arrival of a newcomer to the Village also posed a threat. I was not a bully, and I tried desperately to avoid being the target of the few tyrants in our small community. I had to take all this into consideration every time I played games or even rode my bike down the street.

Certain families were huge in size by today's standards. Their branches contained no less than ten to fifteen members of all ages, sizes and temperaments. On the outside and walking a thin chalk line was Candy. Despite numerous bouts of whining to beg admittance as a "play-cousin," she spent the majority of her childhood facing one family group or another completely alone.

In every community there is a sin that is classified by the inhabitants as being the most horrible to commit. In those days, unlike the current tumultuous society of the new millennium, murder was a rare occurrence. As far as we knew, it only happened inside the limits of the city of Pittsburgh. By our silently agreed upon definition in the Village, the voluntary participation in "he said, she said" was absolutely the most heinous of sins. "He said, she said" is known in traditional terms as gossip. Honestly, both the children and the adults participated actively in carrying tales from one household to the other. It was proper to talk, but improper to carry hurtful rumors. Carrying one of these bitter pills against your neighbor could bring down upon the head of the sinner the wrath of the entire Village.

Should a child decide to practice "he said, she said" it was certain the family of the subject of the story would unite against them. On their side would stand the very parents of the gossiper. Often the parent would have a switch in their hands ready to thrash the living daylights out of the sinner. The level of punishment did not in any way depend on whether or not the "he said, she said" was true or false. The end result was that the sinner received at least several embarrassing threats from their peers and sometimes faced one or two physical altercations as a result of his stupidity.

The family to which I belonged was mostly composed of adults. Jerry was my one and only male playmate-cousin. In fact, we were the same age. Immediately after school, I was expected to report to his house to wait for my mother to retrieve me on her way home from work. I called his mother Aunt Gert. Their white aluminum shingled house was right in the middle of the Village. Aunt Gert spent numerous hours nurturing the many varieties of flowers that lined the stairwell to the home. She prided herself in being a professional housewife who loved to listen to the Pittsburgh Pirates and Friday night Gillette sponsored boxing matches. Her favorite simple pastime was to spend warm summer evenings entertaining close friends on her green well-maintained front porch.

Pennsylvania winters could extend for four months or more. The temperatures were capable of dipping below zero Fahrenheit and were generally wet and nasty. At first, the snow was beautiful. When it mixed with the freezing rain, it became a nuisance. In those days, I remember always feeling cold. Our house in the gully had only a pot-bellied stove. Cousin Jerry's house was heated by a huge furnace which provided warmth to each room via a ventilation system.

Aunt Gert was an organized woman that believed you should be completely comfortable sitting on plastic covered furniture. Every family picture and ashtray was given a specific placement assignment on the mantle above her unused fireplace. Dust was outlawed in her house. Every corner of her yard was an important part of a neatly cut and trimmed presentation. The chores were performed by a reluctant cleaning and cutting crew. It consisted of her two sons and too often I was commissioned to perform some chore that I considered meaningless. This assignment usually involved the use of a broom or mop. She did not tolerate dirty feet anywhere in the home. I rarely was allowed to go upstairs to the family bedrooms because it was in her mind, somewhere I had "no business."

Jerry was by all standards a child with many advantages. I tried desperately to share his expensive toys and the heat from his favorite vent. It irritated me that he selfishly insisted on laying right in front of the warm vent to watch TV every evening. I was so cold on the plastic covers on the sofa that I felt like begging him to share the heat. Most of the time, he acted like I wasn't even in the room. In general, he always managed to avoid conversations. He didn't seem to be at all interested in anything I tried to share with him. Most of the time, he only tolerated my existence. Infrequently and without any explanation, he threatened to beat the crap out of me. In order to enforce this threat, he would shove me as far away from his prized vent as possible.

On one occasion, when we were six or seven, for no reason he simply walked around a corner of the house and punched me in the face. I ran to the back porch and screamed in anguish to get the attention of Aunt Gert. For this infraction he was sent to a cherry tree in the middle of the yard to pick not one, but two switches. She taunted and at the same time thrashed him as I watched, pouted and gloated.

In addition to the switching, he was restricted to his room for two weeks. His unprovoked blow had left a red and swollen mark on my face that seemed to work in my favor. Aunt Gert, for an extended period, added extra peanut butter to my afternoon sandwich. The first day after the incident she even gave me more of her precious Welch's Concord Grape Preserves than usual. For the first time I was allowed to enjoy all the benefits of the vent, my cousin's exotic toys and the TV without interruption.

Despite this and more disagreements, it was understood in the Village street that we were one of the family units.

Each day the feelings of permanence and stability carefully cultivated for us by our proud parents naturally and gently eroded at a predictable rate. It was a factor that could not be blamed only on a war or any other single catastrophic event. Rapidly changing and violent social events of the decade and the related fear became the catalysts that would partially result in my generation's voluntary separation from the Village. A disappointing side effect was to be the fragmentation of several large family units.

CHAPTER 5 -- AN EMPTY HOUSE

At an early age, it is normal to begin the practice of classifying friends. In business a person is an associate if you only have to see them over lunch or in a meeting. The bullies of our Village were therefore childhood associates with whom I shared a ride on the school bus. The rest of the time I did everything possible to avoid them. My fear of confrontations with the ever changing hierarchy of bullies did not prevent me from enjoying countless hours directly involved in the very hectic lives of the other huge Village familiar units.

Two ways existed for me to get from the house in the gully to the street that ran through the middle of the Village. If I went up the wooden steps my father diligently maintained, I still had a walk of another 3 blocks to cover before I'd arrive at the divisive bush at the bottom of the main street of the Village. During my younger years, it was easier to take a shortcut that wound its way through the wooded steep banks of the gully. Marilyn's house was at the exit of the shortcut. She was to become one of my first friends.

Marilyn's sleek dark looks and bright eyes seemed to have an effect on everyone she met. She and her younger brother were a part of the Village when we were all too young to realize the importance of a family association. I preferred to make the journey during the late summer mornings and usually I'd find Marilyn playing along the side of her house with my other friend, Savannah. As a child of only 7, I had absolutely no knowledge of the state of Georgia and therefore no appreciation for Savannah's long first name. So, we all simply called her Vannie. Vannie had many brothers and sisters and she was a member of absolutely the largest Village family.

The times we played together as young children were simple and precious. This was probably because all that was important was that we liked each other. We didn't always agree on what we wanted to do and there were times Marilyn preferred not to participate in the more tom-boyish activities. Sometimes, we'd play house. Marilyn or Vannie would recruit a younger sibling to be the baby. Or we'd make mud pies and serve exquisite tea with rock cookies as we pretended to be ladies. The older girls of the Village preferred that we entertain ourselves. They constantly reminded us that we were too small to remember the verses of the rhymes required to jump rope. Lacking adequate eye-hand coordination, we also couldn't play jacks. The game of jacks was played with a small red rubber ball and tiny colored metal stars. It was the most popular game of that era.

One day I was informed that Marilyn's father had gotten a new job in a place called Connecticut. By this time, we had been close friends for a period of over three years. This is a long time in the life of a child. Vannie and I knew that Marilyn would be leaving. However, I don't think either one of us had a true grasp of the magnitude of the event. Once we were given the news, we did the natural thing any child would do. We continued to play and act as if nothing was going to happen. But that day did come. When Vannie and I ventured to Marilyn's house that sunny midday in April, we found it empty. A moving van parked in the road outside the house now held the table from her mother's kitchen on which we'd often shared milk and cookies. Together Vannie and I stood waving at the tail-end of Marilyn's family car while tears streamed down our faces. We realized that she would now be living in that foreign place called Connecticut. Above all, Marilyn would not be here with us where she really belonged. It was our first taste of the hopelessness that accompanies change and always resides somewhere just beyond the sphere which you control.

It appeared to me that the departure of Marilyn had a greater impact on Vannie. I simply refused to talk about it and sulked for a few days on the branch of a big apple tree in my front yard. Finally, I gathered all the courage I could and I climbed the hill of the gully. I exited in the back of what had been Marilyn's house. We had enjoyed tea parties on the short cement wall next to the house many times. I leaned on the wall and then stood in the yard for some time simply trying to deal with the emptiness that now seemed to seep from each window of the house. The building was now only a strange and hollow place. After a while, the entire thing became too sad to bear alone. I decided to start searching the neighborhood for Vannie.

Vannie's cousins lived almost next door to Marilyn's old house. Their kind mother always dispensed cookies to any child that dropped by her crowded and often chaotic home. I politely called from the door step and she invited me to come upstairs to the kitchen. As I started up the steps Sam suddenly appeared at the top of the steps. He was her middle son and the arch enemy of all the girls in the Village. As was his custom, and for no logical reason, he charged right at me. I quickly moved to one side and ducked. He stumbled his way down the remainder of the stairs. I just ignored his spineless efforts and continued to the kitchen to chat with his mother. In a voice quiet enough not to be heard by his mother, he issued the usual baseless threats of retaliation as he waved his boney fists at me to demonstrate his level of frustration.

The conversation and cookie she and I shared combined to make me feel a bit better. For some reason, I still felt it was important to find Vannie. Her family lived on the bottom floor of the only apartment building in the Village. On the other side of her unit was the watering hole frequented by my father and other men of the Village.

Vannie's immediate family consisted of over seven people. Their home, like that of her cousin's, was crowded and constantly busy. I was always welcomed. In those days you did not ramble about in another person's house even if they asked you to come in. I politely stood in the doorway and asked if anyone had seen Vannie. Numerous voices replied from all directions, "Nope, sorry." By now the temperature had started to rise. Because I was thirsty I decided to go to

Jerry's house in hopes of being offered a tall glass of Kool-Aid from the pitcher that was always full in Aunt Gert's kitchen.

Aunt Gert had chosen this day to prepare fresh, cold lemonade. I was instructed to drink it on the front porch as she handed me a refreshing ice-cold glass filled to the brim. I went around the side of the house the same way I had done the day Jerry slapped me in the face. Just as I sat down to enjoy a sip of the cool liquid, out of the corner of my eye, I saw a laughing Vannie having what looked like a real good time with of all people Candy. I was completely confused. The tears started to fill my eyes. For the first time in my life I felt the pangs of self-pity. There stood my friend in the middle of the street enjoying the company of someone we both had said many times was absolutely peculiar. Candy was beside herself with glee and she giggled and giggled. Now it seemed she had finally become a "play-cousin" to one of the family units through an unpredictable relationship with my friend.

I confess to being upset by this situation for a few weeks. Finally, I realized the whole thing was probably beyond the ability of even a genius to explain. What had made my friend behave in such a strange way? Had I done something wrong that caused me now to be without my oldest friend? Vannie began to spend all her spare time with Candy. I did not even try to compete for her attention. I finally was able to except the situation by concluding that due to the grief and confusion of Marilyn's departure a depressed Vannie had simply taken leave of her senses. The price to play with Vannie was now too high for me to pay. I refused to accept the added expense of putting up with Candy.

Illustrated by Deanna Graves 2012.

CHAPTER 6 -- SERVING GOD AND COUNTRY

My overall health continued to improve. In fact, whenever my mother recounted the story of my beginnings she would always have to assure the listener that the robust chubby girl in front of them was truly the child she had saved. I began to wish she'd just stop telling the story. It seemed that with each telling, I grew less and less confident of my place as a daughter in her home.

I was encouraged to broaden my interests by participating in a Brownie troop in which girls of the Village and the neighborhood combined to undertake many years of cookie sales and badge acquisitions. We worked as a unit. Many of the white mothers volunteered as scout leaders. They seemed to take an equal interest in all members of our troop. For a while, it was almost as if there really wasn't any difference between being white or colored.

It was also at this time that my mother-cousin began to seriously emphasize the fact that I was not really her daughter. Often she would say, "We love you and want to protect you, but you have to accept that we are not your parents. Your real mother and father didn't want you." She told me repeatedly that she would never take me around any of the relatives of my real mother. Whenever she talked about them, it was to emphasize her determination to keep me away from their negative influence. It was as if she wanted me to believe in my new life with her, but not believe in it too much. I wasn't an argumentative child. Therefore, I tried to do exactly what she seemed to want me to do. I attempted to put the unknown past behind me. This left me without a foundation. Without a beginning, I found it almost impossible to believe in a future. A look in the mirror each morning only served to remind me that with my light-skinned appearance I could not possibly be the real daughter of my dark complexioned new parents.

One day she began to add bits of information such as, "Your mother is a strange woman and you'd be better off if you never met her. I don't want to say too much about her except I will say that you shouldn't ever even think about going around her."

The first time I was exposed to this unexpected revelation I ran from the house into the vast wasteland that surrounded the crooked house in the gully. There I sat for hours beneath the stars amongst the worthless vegetation creating games that I desperately hoped would help me to stop feeling completely alone and totally afraid.

Every day, I fought hard to feel appreciative for my good fortune. Instead, the feelings of insecurity continued to grow. Often, I hid away in my room because I couldn't hold back the tears. I didn't want my new parents to think that I was ungrateful. I tried to substitute for the insecurity by putting everything I had into my activities with the Brownies.

The scouting lessons were simple and delivered in a kind manner. We were given personal attention by the leaders of the troop. These women were mostly the mothers of our white schoolmates. They inspired all of us to enjoy ourselves while doing the best job we could at any task. I began to believe that it was important for me to feel proud to be an American. We sang encouraging songs and memorized the treasured Girl Scout Pledge, "On my honor, I will try, to do my duty to God and my country, to help other people at all times, and to obey the Girl Scout Law."

During the hour long sessions I remained attentive, but in my heart I lacked the confidence to attempt to socialize with my peers. The scout leaders always tried to inspire me to mingle. They often asked, "Jean, don't you want to sit over here with the rest of the girls while we work on our project?"

At this point, I usually lowered my head, and nodded in agreement. Reluctantly, I forced myself to join the group. I struggled to laugh at what I thought were the right times. Deep inside there was nothing I could do to stop feeling alienated and unwanted. The world renowned cookie campaigns were exciting times for the troop members and our families. The white members of the exclusive sector of our community were accepting and supportive of our efforts. They encouraged us to place our posters in advance in the storefront windows. Usually, I made the commitment to accept more boxes than I could possibly ever sell. I looked forward to the door to door sales as an opportunity to actually go up on the porches of the beautiful houses in the neighborhood.

One day, Vannie and I decided to work together in order to cover a rather large street in the neighborhood. It was a crisp, clear day without a cloud in the sky. We had tried to concentrate on the task at hand. Instead, we found ourselves mixing the sales effort with fun and games. Neither one of us had a watch but we realized we should return home soon. Vannie was beside herself with pride. She had sold more boxes of cookies than me.

"How many do you think we'll sell today?" asked Vannie as she rearranged the cookies in her double paper bag with handles.

"I don't know because I've never tried to sell anything on this street before," I replied.

Unfortunately, I had too much experience in sales around the neighborhood since responding to an article in the back of a popular periodical. The enticing ad promised me I could at least double my initial investment of $2.00. I honestly saw myself as successful. In my mind I envisioned all the extra goodies I'd purchase with my profits. With this sense of confidence, I didn't feel it was necessary to inform my mother. I decided to wait until after I had quickly sold out of the wonderful salve and actually had the profits in my hand to show her.

The yellow, sweet smelling salve was described as being an all-purpose product that could ease pain and suffering in addition to acting as a protection for sensitive skin. I had neglected to read the fine print. Soon, the first shipment of 24 tins was followed by another 12. I lost all the accumulated savings from my modest allowance money to this enterprise. Shortly after I received the second shipment, the harassing letters began to arrive demanding even more money. My mother begrudgingly paid for two more shipments. I only managed to sell a total of 3 tins. The household inherited a lifetime supply of the multi-purpose gunk. My practical father often used it to lubricate his set of Sears' Craftsman wrenches.

"We'd better hurry up. You take that side of the street and I'll take this one," said Vannie as she fought to balance her purse from a long strap on one arm and the paper bag on the other. I avoided carrying purses and preferred to keep anything of value that would fit in one of my socks.

For some reason, I felt confident while approaching strangers. Disappointment never occurred to me even if I didn't sell one box. After all, this was not just a challenge to convince someone you didn't know to buy something from you. This was my one opportunity to get a really good look at the well cared for plants that adorned the porches and front yards of the lots in the neighborhood. To my delight, I sometimes managed to glimpse inside the homes. I was fascinated by the shining wooden floors and gleaming crystal chandeliers inside the alcoves.

Vannie's late sales drive seemed to be a brilliant idea. I observed her digging into her purse in an attempt to find change on several occasions. On the other hand, I had only sold 2 more boxes of cookies after approaching four homes.

We continued to go from door to door for the better part of a half hour. I was by this time totally distracted and content with the modest sale of 6 boxes while Vannie's sales had soared and she now only had a few boxes left.

"I'm going to do one more house. I bet I can get rid of the rest of these right over there." She pointed to a house which set neatly on a corner lot.

"Heck, I'm tired and I'll wait for you across the street." At this point I started to look around for a comfortable place to sit and wait.

Just as Vannie started to walk towards the house, another fellow scout from the Village came around the corner. She too only had a few boxes left to sell and she asked Vannie if they could go together to this last house.

The two were comparing their sales and laughing. I watched them and quietly adjusted the hemline of my skirt. I wanted to make sure that it would cover my knees as I sat down on a raised stone wall of another residence across the street from the targeted home. A warm wind rustled my brown sash with metals. My lightly starched brown skirt and white blouse still looked neat after wearing them for so many hours. I felt a sense of pride despite having sold fewer boxes than I anticipated. Above all, I had managed to catch a peek inside many of the homes I treasured. Today had been an overall success.

The contentment I felt was soon to be disrupted as I observed some peculiar behavior on the part of Vannie and the other scout. The resident of the home was now on the porch in front of them shouting. My friends continued to stand directly in front of him as he kept repeating the same phrase over and over again, "Get your nigger asses out of here!"

I was too startled to move. The blatant hatred in the man's total demeanor frightened me. I'd seen this man at the grocery store and in other places throughout the area. I never thought that it was possible that he held so much contempt against colored people. Vannie and the other scout continued to stand bravely in front of him. Finally, he seemed to realize he was not making much progress with the two girls. He continued to level ugly explicates while working his way back into his house.

When the man entered the home he slammed the door so hard I thought the glass panes on that whole side of the house would break. At this point, the two girls slowly left the porch. I knew there was nothing I could do to help my friends. It was the first time in my life I was truly afraid. I was shocked to recall later that for some reason I did not run or start to cry. I remained frozen on the hard bricks trying to resist the horrible desire to flee for my life that was growing in the pit of my stomach.

It wasn't the first time that I'd seen an adult appear to be consumed by anger. Nor would this be the last. It also wasn't the first time I heard the word nigger being used to try to humiliate either me or someone else from the Village. I was shocked and confused because I just couldn't accept the fact that the man didn't understand the really good reason we were trying to sell cookies. Why didn't he realize that we were good American Girl Scouts who wanted to live up to our oath? Vannie did not appear to be frightened. Instead she was obviously just as angry as the insulting persecutor she'd just confronted.

"People around here make me sick. Who does he think he is?" She kept repeating these phrases over and over again as we walked back to the Village.

Two things had permanently changed. No matter how hard I tried I no longer looked forward to the annual cookie sales. Vannie to me now seemed to be much older and wiser.

"I am going to do one more house. I bet I can get rid of these right over there." Illustrated by Deanna Graves 2012.

CHAPTER 7 -- THE HORDE

It was at this time a new family with ties to Sam moved into a home very close to the gully. There were countless members of this tribe, and each year it seemed another baby was brought into the world from within their ranks. The ages of the children ranged from less than a year all the way to twenty. All of the ones my age were girls. They made it well known that if anyone dared to offend any one of them the end result for the violator would be painful and very unpleasant.

The new social situation in the Village became a challenge because I had to find a non-disruptive way to continue to play the games I loved so much without becoming the focus of retaliation for the massive family. The most difficult obstacle to forming a peaceful co-existence with the horde of new arrivals was that their favorite excuse for reprisal was almost always based on "he said, she said." One member or another would stand in the street and declare before God and the entire Village, "I heard what you said about my sister." They then worked themselves into a fevered state by performing the tribe's ritual dance before the hunt began for the offender. The dance consisted of loudly repeating the "he said, she said" information between their members until their voices could be heard from within all the houses in the Village.

The persecution suffered by so many members of the Village at the hands of the tribe of new arrivals for the most part did not affect me. In order to endure and still function with the new Village order, I developed a persona based on the stern application of caution. I did not ride my bike within the Village and I only made an appearance on the street just before the captains chose sides for the evening kickball games. The horde never knew what I thought about them because I did not hold personal conversations with any other child in the Village. One of the new rules of my behavior included finding a way to escape into the early evening shadows before the customary chiding of the losers began. The horde was never content with the result of any game played even if it had been conducted using their set of rules. Therefore, if I wanted to avoid being involved in the inevitable confrontation, my only option was to disappear. I admit to resorting to prayer on many occasions. I promised God anything if he kept them from finding some twisted reason to fling themselves upon me before I could safely reach the door of my house in the gully.

It was not my behavior but that of my father that set the horde on a hunt for me. One day I was surrounded during a routine walk to the A&P grocery store at the edge of the neighborhood. While taking turns pushing and shoving me around like a rag doll, they repeatedly advised me, "We know what your father said about my sister." I was too shocked to respond in any way because my father was probably the least offensive person in the Village. For some reason, they did not actually decide to beat me within an inch of my life. The last thing that each uttered over and over as they left me stunned and shaken was, "Tell that old man we're gonna' kick his ass."

When I finally found my father and recounted the entire event, he calmly said, "I hope those stupid girls do try something." He never explained to me what he thought about their "he said, she said" claims. Instead, he only added, "Let me know if they bother you again."

I always suspected that my father was the embodiment of the famous words of Teddy Roosevelt. He was a small man who did; "Speak softly and carry a big stick." It was either this philosophy or his WWI experiences that kicked-in to save us. He seemed to accomplish something the rest of the Village only dreamed of achieving. The short, soft-spoken man somehow stopped the horde's hunt for vengeance. It is still a mystery as to what he had actually said that launched their fit of retaliation or how he accomplished the miracle of appeasement. The end result was that the horde no longer seemed interested in my activities. I was able to enjoy an increased level of exposure and began to try to reclaim old ties and establish some sort of normal existence.

A couple of years of horde imposed dominance had transpired during which I had adhered to a lonely and rigid lifestyle. This change in my behavior seemed to render me invisible to my former playmates. It was impossible to compete for the now lost friendship with Vannie. Her relationship with Candy appeared to now be as solid as a rock. In desperation and jealousy, I did one day attack Candy. Unprovoked, I jumped on her back and beat her from the middle of the street to the base of the stairs that lead to her house. I continued to hit her in the back and pull her long thick braids while warning her that an even more severe beating would be dealt to her if she informed on me to any of the Village parents. Therefore, I was able to savor the enjoyment of my revenge without the troublesome fear of punishment.

My state of euphoria lasted for only a couple of days. Shortly after the confrontation with Candy, retribution was extracted from me by one of our most infamous bullies, Niece. I was given a black eye, a blow to the head and more than a few sore ribs for an unrelated incident centering around Niece's resentment to the tone of my voice. She believed in being "respected." During a basketball game, she took offense to my protest of a call by her of a ball as being out of play. I found myself on the ground right beside the ball before I could even think about defending myself. The only thing she said to me, as she waved her fist fiercely in front of my face was, "Now, that is out of bounds, bitch!"

CHAPTER 8 -- GOING TO CHURCH

The most important thing to do after you learned to walk was to hone your newly found skill by applying it as you and your friends made your way to church. Attendance was mandatory. As soon as a child of the Village protested the required Sunday pilgrimage he was advised, "When you're so grown you think you can stop going to church you will also be grown enough to leave this house!" The adults of the Village absolutely lacked any sense of humor about going to church.

Traditionally, the older children were designated as leaders and it was their task to watch over the smaller children as the group walked through the neighborhood. The parents always gave us money to put in church. Often, they added a little extra to be used for a special treat after services at Isley's Ice Cream Parlor.

Saturday night and Sunday morning the parents concentrated on our appearance. The ritual would start with a good Saturday evening scrubbing and preparation of the "Sunday and funeral" only clothing. Little girls, who preferred to roll down mud hills on cardboard boxes or play with mud pies, found themselves sitting in front of their mother or older sister on the floor while their hair sizzled as it was straightened, plaited and oiled. Within most homes of the Village you could always find a big jar of Vaseline. This was used all over the body in order to avoid "looking ashy." Families with few children sometimes purchased lotions and even talcum powder. In order to make your hair shine all it took was a little bit of Dixie Peach or Royal Crown.

The boys for the most part escaped the pre-church process. They only had to stand still Sunday morning while their parents almost lifted them out of their shoes as they tucked in their shirttails and firmly brushed their freshly clipped hair.

It was not possible to feel comfortable in the "Sunday and funeral" clothes. The dresses were made of cotton or frilly chiffon and usually had some sort of lace trim. Under the dresses little girls who were ladies wore petti coats. Generally, all the clothing for boys and girls was purchased in a size larger then required so that the frock could be used for more than one year. For the girls, this translated to mean that a new dress was usually so big that safety pins had to be attached to the petti coats to keep the oversized garment from falling off. The hope for a change of clothing held by all the children was based on the fact that one day even the most resilient garment became too short or too tight to wear. Village families with many daughters passed the dresses down the line without the need for alterations. If a dress was of good quality and after at least two years of qualified Sunday-only wear, the dress then became a school dress for the remainder of its tour of duty. Absolutely nothing went to waste. "Waste not, want not" was one of the Village mottos.

Special mention was given to the gross patent leather shoes preferred by the adults of the Village for their daughters. The shoes would squeak and grind as you walked. Their 100% leather soles made it possible to fall without warning on any surface and at any time. Patent leather shoes should be avoided because they do not provide airflow. We were forced to wear them every Sunday despite the proven fact that as you wear them they actually contract. One strong selling point to these shoes was that it was very easy to extend their lifespan. Wise parents purchased them a bit too large and temporarily filled the available space by adding crumpled newspaper. The heels were given taps and the soles re-done as many times as necessary.

So, it was that we suffered, squeaked and tried desperately not to stumble our way to Sunday school. Sunday school was held in the basement and the adult Sunday school met upstairs. The children practiced songs and memorized scriptures while struggling to keep their "Sunday-funeral" clothes clean. Within the first few minutes of class, the Dixie Peach lubricated plaits started to unwind and the patent leather shoes began to shrink. Although we knew this was just the beginning of at least a full three to four more hours of discomfort, we clenched our teeth or sometimes outright started to cry in order to at least disturb the monotony. It was not permissible to wiggle in your seat, pick you teeth or nose, twist your hair or the hair of someone else, or do anything that required movement.

The boys had arrived ready to leave. The teacher solved this problem by rotating the snickering young men and sometimes even the young women in and out of the isolated time out corner near the back of the room.

    Suddenly, from the floor above we began to hear a rumble. The adults had ended their morning service. Now they were singing one of those old chants they had learned as children in the South. This "warm-up" service was usually attended by the really devoted members. We knew that it would soon be time to go upstairs. Each one of us feared and wondered exactly what the teacher would tell our parents about our behavior in Sunday school. The sounds of church increased and the "amens," "thank you Lords" were being uttered closer and closer together. It was at this time that the acappella singing of the great black classics by the old deacons echoed throughout the church. The deacons knew exactly when to pound their feet to keep the rhythm, and often the sounds they uttered resembled moans.

    The teacher passed the collection plate and we obediently gave our expected donations. This would be our first exposure to financial guilt and exasperation. During the regular service, we knew to expect at least two or three more offerings upstairs. If we were skillful enough to avoid contributing to even one offering, we would have enough left of our allowance to purchase a double scoop ice cream cone. Sometimes the preacher's sermon was designed to make the congregation feel ashamed of the size of their tithe or other donation. The message was powerfully delivered. It was impossible to avoid the eyes of the adults. At times like these, I usually gave the church my last cent.

Often, the Sunday school sponsored a special fund raising campaign. The children were told to take home flat cardboard cards. Each card contained circles cut out the size of pennies, or dimes or even quarters. We were directed to insert all our "extra money" into the slots.

Once the cards were full they were supposed to be returned to the teacher. In this way, the children could personally help pay some of the expenses of the Sunday school. Frankly, we rarely had any money. In some cases, we were able to earn an allowance from our parents. The allowance was not earned simply by completing chores. The chores must be inspected and approved, while maintaining good grades and only if you continuously cleaned your plate of every crumb at every meal. It was not uncommon for the entire allowance to be denied if a disciplinary infraction of any kind occurred or an assigned task was left undone. The Village parents did not play games with their hard earned money.

If we actually earned any allowance, we used the precious funds to buy candy and potato chips after school. The amount of an average allowance was never much more than the twenty-two cent cost in those days of a loaf of bread. It was a mystery to us how we were supposed to fill the ten or twelve slots on each of the Sunday school donation cards. The truth was that the parents took charge of the cards. Our only true responsibility was to be sure the cardboard challenge safely reached our homes. Once there, they were filled by our elders and we promptly returned them within the allotted time to our teacher. Logic dictates that the cards were intended for our parents all along. The Church was very good at raising money. Unlike a bill collector, the institution was more than capable of extracting "blood out of a turnip."

After the donation plate was collected, we lined-up at the bottom of the steps in order to go upstairs where we would join the rest of the congregation. By this time, the pianist had arrived and the walls began to vibrate. The air above our heads was filled with the rhythmic pounding of feet, the vigorous clapping of hands and the singing and shouting of the faithful. This house of God truly believed and practiced "making a joyful noise unto the Lord."

If it was a Communion Sunday, we knew the service would last at least an additional hour. It was at this time that the girls' socks started to slip inside the plastic feeling shoes. Frequently, we'd have to bend over in order to perform a sock adjustment. The most important thing to do as we joined the congregation was to make sure we did not have to sit beside certain "sanctified" members. There were ladies and some men of the church that were known to jump out their seats as they danced and sometimes even spoke in different "tongues." It was never obvious when they would erupt into celebration or which direction they would take because they were "filled with the Holy Spirit." We tried to stay out of their way and only wanted the day to be over.

The adults were proud of their young pastor and they seemed to like his older and shy wife. He was a short, neat man who constantly had to adjust his glasses. In those days the ministers did not mince words. He was quick to criticize the congregation for many things. The children had been warned that the pastor had eyes and ears everywhere. He knew everybody's business. His frequent sermons about hell and damnation brought fear into our eyes. The Pastor admonished the members to be generous with their time and money as it related to the church. A tithe was considered to be a 10% before tax obligation. This contribution was a guaranteed subject of at least one sermon each and every month.

Prayers were offered by the church for the sick. The infrequent visitors were welcomed and encouraged to testify. Their confessions and often tearful sentiments would sometimes cause the choir to break into another two or three moving choruses. The competency of the choir depended on which members were present.

As if on cue, it was at this point that most of the children began to start to feel sleepy. It was not advisable to be caught napping. The petticoats had started to fall beneath the hemlines of our dresses and we continued to fight the futile battle against the ever falling socks and the noisy shoes.

After singing and shouting with his choir and calling for the first two collection plates, the preacher was now more than ready to deliver the message of the day. He launched into the sermon by shouting in the traditional sing-song way, "Yessss Lord, it is a good day. All God's children say Amen."

Gradually, to emphasis portions of the message the volume of his voice increased and he'd stomp his foot, clap his hands and pace back and forth in front of the podium. The Reverend's tone and manner was that of a typical black preacher of his era. His delivery came in waves of half-sung, half-chanted phrases. The adults encouraged him. Sometimes, they would suddenly spring from their seats to shout, "Amen, you tell it preacher." "Hallelujah." "Thank you Lord!"

Some of the "sanctified" members had long ago left their seats. Usually, during his sermon there were those that even fainted. You could easily tell where they had fallen by looking for the sisters of the church. These devoted ladies always proudly wore white uniforms and they carried large handkerchiefs with lace borders. When the sanctified tumbled, these sisters could be seen waving fans, or wiping their brows in an effort to revive them.

We continued to fight off sleep while the church thundered.

The Preacher's voice began to soften and the pianist inched her way from her seat with the choir to the piano. As the preacher ended his sermon, she began to play. He lifted his hand in the air and called his flock to the altar. Most of the congregation had been baptized by this same preacher, so it was rare that anyone answered his summons to "go to the water." Someone seeking a special blessing or with a desire to officially join the church would stand and move forward. The preacher whispered and chatted with the one in need. After another song of celebration for the delivery of this poor soul, there still could be a request for another collection. Finally, the church was dismissed as the congregation chanted together, "And the Lord watch over me and thee while we are absent one from another. Amen."

The braver of us actually tried to run out the church even before the last words of the dismissal chant were uttered. In our minds we felt justified because we had been still three or four hours. All we could think about was that if a special event was planned for a service in the evening we would have to return in less than two hours to once again be required to sit still for what could at least be another two or three more hours. This left little time to spend the dime at the ice cream parlor and less time to try to enjoy a traditional and bountiful Sunday dinner.

Up the hill from the church was the beloved ice cream parlor, Isaly's. The shop was a branch of a larger chain and it offered all sorts of special dairy treats. The older Village children supervised the purchase of the ice cream cones and they began to monitor themselves and their charges to avoid spills on the "Sunday and funeral" clothing. In small satellite groups, we began our walk through a cool, wooded park at the edge of the neighborhood.

We knew exactly what awaited us on top of our mothers' stoves. Wise women of the Village always prepared most of the Sunday dinner in advance. The meal on Sunday was almost as special as the ones served for the holidays. A pleasant and comforting aroma reached out to greet us somewhere close to the divisive hedge. Fried chicken, roast beef with lots of onions, chicken and dumplings, sweet potatoes, mixed greens and fresh cornbread. The smells mixed together and called us to our homes.

It should be mentioned that many of the Village adults did not attend church. This was not because they had to work Saturday or Sunday. In those days, the vast majority of businesses out of a respect for God, the employee and public opinion remained closed the entire weekend. We did not dare ask our parents why they or one of their peers avoided attending church. It was well understood that a child should "stay in their place." This place was definitely in a position nowhere close to "grown folk's business." The exclusive "grown folk's business" seemed to be a vast subject and we always wondered when we would be qualified to listen. The day of sharing the restricted knowledge never arrived. The adults of the Village retained their elevated position and exclusive information even after we were grown.

CHAPTER 9 -- THE IMPORTANCE OF ICE CREAM

The health of my adopted parents began to fade as I entered my teen years. Many of the older children had gone off to college or for one reason or another they'd decided to leave the Village to begin a new life. After my twelfth birthday, my adoptive mother was often too tired or sick to help me prepare for Church. Therefore, it became my task to do all that was necessary Saturday evening. By now, there was cold running water in the house from the spring. Unfortunately, we still relied on the outside toilet. I took charge of the Vaseline and Dixie Peach and promptly woke myself up in time to attend Sunday school every Sunday morning.

The amount of the allowances and church allotments had greatly increased as had our ability to avoid the guilt associated with not sharing our increase with the always demanding preacher. Instead of just an ice cream cone that now sold for almost a quarter, we were able to afford chips, pop and candy.

Some of the older children, who were by now young adults, took pride in volunteering to be Sunday school teachers. As a child at their knees, I knew them all too well. Some had been tyrants when they led the smaller children to and from church. Perhaps they had mistakenly thought that this new position of authority would naturally be respected by the children. Most would be driven to resign due to the many pranks and inability to control the behavior of their siblings. Others stood their ground and found themselves humbled by the experience.

I vividly recall hearing my mother singing "Precious Lord" from the kitchen as I went off to church. She was one of those that seldom attended the small church she insisted I go to at the edge of the neighborhood. Instead, she would catch a ride on the trolley and go into the city and find her own way to celebrate the Lord. Sometimes, I felt that her love of God and the consuming worship of Him were the only things that kept her going. It was a complicated long-suffering and tolerant religion that she practiced. The only constants were her singing of the same old hymns, the heart-felt verbalizations of faith and a determined devotion to God. After rushing to eat dinner I would sometimes follow this nomadic, strong woman on her quest to find the perfect house in which to worship the Lord.

Often this "call to worship" led her to attend all types of churches. One year, she preferred a sanctified assembly several trolley transfers from the Village. Then, the next year she attended numerous tent meetings held by a rebellious, "jack-legged" preacher. The "jack-legged" preachers were rebels who under protest had dramatically resigned from a junior pastor position with a large church. They seldom left alone and were often followed by a portion of the large church's congregation.

I still find confusing the questionable attitude of the parents about church. We heard them often criticize their peers for not giving enough to the Lord. The children of the village knew everyone's business because the adults thought that we were as we should be, seen but not heard. In all fairness, they cannot be held responsible for the period type and style of clothing that we suffered to wear. They are at least in part accountable for the never-ending skepticism of their children as it relates to the church.

In later years, the congregation discovered that the Pastor had been more than a bit self-serving regarding the spending of the church money. It is reasonable to believe that somewhere within the forbidden "grown-folks" business there was the knowledge that explained the preacher's expensive habits. He wore fine suits and drove new cars despite being shepherd to a flock that floundered on the edge of poverty.

The most important thing to relate is the effect all this forced attendance may have had upon me and my peers. The majority of us seem to have tried to maintain some sort of relationship with a preferred religious institution and with the Lord. Almost universally, we confess to being at best only reluctant contributors to the coffers of religious institutions. The memory of the preacher from our past seems to have mingled with the observed actions of several of his greedy Christian brothers we've encountered as adults.

Because of the struggling and insistence of our parents we managed to become almost universally a well-educated generation. Therefore, many of us proudly claim a different level of sophistication. For the most part, we would not in any way behave as if we are sanctified. Yet, there is still an appreciation and a deep love in our hearts for the old songs, and a God that will "never fail." No matter how far we strayed from the Village or how infrequent our trips to one of God's houses, most of us have found it soothing to incorporate the simple habit of buying ice cream after church into our lives as we raised our own children.

CHAPTER 10 -- A PERFECT RECIPE

Everyone is entitled to believe they are capable of doing one thing better than anyone else. It was a shame and disgrace in the Village if you were a woman and couldn't handle yourself in the kitchen. Some recipes were shared and others are now buried with their prideful creators. Dealing with food was viewed as an art and exact science. The competitions didn't have to be advertised on the radio and the judges were taken from amongst the ranks of the husbands, the children and flow of never-ending real or "play cousins" that were always visiting in the home of the cook.

The ladies spent long hours scouring the *Pittsburgh Post Gazette* and the *Pittsburgh Courier* for unique ways to deal with common food items. Each edition of Ebony magazine featured a new approach to a down-home favorite and it was for this reason as much as the magazines strong fashion sense that assured a copy could be found in almost every Village home. Chatting about the effects of one spice or another on a favorite cut of meat could consume hours. There were times that the end result of the attempts at culinary uniqueness found its only home in the dish used to feed the dog on the back porch. It was a clean competition and the only prize was a sense of satisfaction tapered by modest bragging rights.

The categories included canning, pickling, frying, baking and barbecuing. Every holiday and special event brought out another unofficial clash of champions. Exotic spices that couldn't be obtained at the A&P at the edge of the neighborhood were acquired during shopping expeditions to downtown Pittsburgh. The old city marketplace smelled of fish, fresh vegetables and fruits mixed together with a dash of garlic and oregano on the side. Special admiration was extended to the Italian and Scandinavian bakeries that surrounded the always crowded facility due to their fabulous presentation of pastries, cakes and crisp fresh breads. A side benefit was that this was another place the ladies were able to acquire new recipes.

An unofficially declared rule was that cherished special food items should demand extended periods of dedicated and tireless preparation. In the meat category the challenge was always a cheap cut of meat known as round steak. Hours of marinating in just the right spice and careful searing sometimes guaranteed it could be eaten. The steak was a tough beast that even the dog sometimes refused to eat. The idea was to get the most out of every dime spent on foodstuffs. The ladies of the Village seemed to agree that in the case of round steak a cook worth her salt should know how to prepare the leathery substance.

Universal respect and praise went to any lady who was able to fry mouthwatering chicken. Some households suffered at the hands of a mother who never really figured-out exactly how hot the grease should be. If the pieces were scorched they would be eaten after scrapping off the burned edges. The solution for an under-cooked platter of chicken was to simply throw the entire batch into the oven to finish the cooking that should've occurred in the frying pan. The most important thing was that it be consumed because absolutely nothing went to waste in the Village.

Late spring and early summer were marked by vigorous canning sessions that started with the picking of the fresh fruit or vegetable. Apples, pears, plums and cherries were plentiful and the members of the Village except one family always shared the bounty from trees that grew only in their yard. Those trees that were off-bounds offered a challenge to the children and the birds. Both frequently conducted raids to acquire the fruit that was selfishly hoarded.

Gardening involved almost everyone in the family. The abundant rich soil required care before and after planting. Planting was a tedious task for which the parents recruited their very reluctant children to do the majority of bending and digging. After the seeds were in the ground, the enemies lined-up one by one, and sometimes together. The bugs and weeds vigorously assaulted the garden. It was all worth it when the crops came in and a tired child could sit on the warm soil and enjoy a fresh radish, onion or carrot.

A trip to the A&P to buy Ball's glass jars and tops was the next task to accomplish. If jelly and jam were to be made a special wax to insert between the jar top and commodity to be preserved also had to be acquired. Every utensil and the jars and lids used to prepare the items had to be thoroughly boiled in a huge pot to prevent contamination. Kitchens became assembly lines and the proud cooks demanded to be left alone so that they could concentrate. The miracle of canning is that almost anything can be pickled. The real trick is to make the batch taste good enough for human consumption.

The ultimate summer culinary challenges were the barbecues. Today these would be called cook-offs, and they generally took place prior to a trip to an amusement park for the school picnic. Ribs and steaks sizzled on grills while we hopelessly begged for samples. This was the only thing left for us to do. After all, the adults did not trust us around an open flame. Usually, the best cuts of meat were the exclusive property of the grown-ups. A skillet was usually placed on the grill so fresh fish could be added to the menu. In the house the mothers packed the huge wicker picnic baskets. This was usually the first opportunity to include a recently canned example of pickled eggs and beets or homemade gherkins.

The Village members always found picnic tables that were close together at the school picnic in West View Park. Adults shared the task of setting the tables after sending the children off to enjoy the arcade and amusement rides. A massive amount of food was liberally displayed and the end result could best be described as a communal banquet.

Summer was the only season in which cooking at the stove or oven was given a holiday. Houses in the Village did not have air conditioning and the old fans and an open window could not cool a house enough to even consider undertaking frying or baking. The ladies took advantage of this respite to perform research and hold evening discussions on front porches regarding two subjects: the behavior of their children and the meals they had enjoyed over the years.

Yeast rolls are a great southern tradition. Usually, these are about two to three inches high and presented after garnishing them with real butter to highlight a festive meal. One year following a trip to visit her cousin in New York, Aunt Gert announced that she had the world's best refrigerator roll recipe. The information received a skeptical acknowledgement from my mother. The claim for preparing the best rolls at every holiday dinner had been rotated between the two proud cooks. In order to strengthen her case Aunt Gert added, "They take at least 3 days to prepare."

The next holiday was Thanksgiving. Aunt Gert hosted the event with flare. She served ham, turkey, sweet potatoes, fresh mixed greens, macaroni and cheese, dressing and my mother's famous potato salad. The entire house smelled of the secret yeast rolls because they were the last to go into the oven. The adults exclusively sat at the table. We children were left to find a place to eat on the stairwell. Aunt Gert extracted the rolls from the oven and doused them liberally with fresh butter. They were an awesome sight because they stood well over a full inch higher than any of their down-home predecessors. Finally, the taste testing would truly tell the story. The rolls were glorious and it is no exaggeration to declare that they simply melted in your mouth.

The rolls and samples of them were dispersed to several of her friends through-out the Village. As the fame of the refrigerator rolls increased, my mother's search for a better recipe was to span years without success. Every single time Aunt Gert prepared the rolls they were perfect. The entire situation drove my mother to carry on experiment after experiment. One day after perhaps five years or more she reluctantly conceded that Aunt Gert's refrigerator rolls truly could not be outdone.

CHAPTER 11 -- THE VIOLIN

The strong Village community entertained and supported each other. This was especially true during the weekends and long summers. There were guidelines and rules which kept the two communities separated that went unsaid. All these regulations were accepted and adhered to without question or hesitation. We all knew they were designed to keep Village residents in their place. The adults seemed to have the same position in society that they assigned to their children. We lived in a community that didn't mind seeing us as long as they didn't have to hear us.

The adults of the Village did suffer as a result of the silent apartheid. Many of the men spent numerous hours at the Village watering hole, or simply remained in the big city after work with their other woman (and sometimes "outside children"). The woman of the Village kept watch from their porches for their husbands to stumble home. Almost every weekend like clockwork, the same Village husband and father would proudly stagger down the street proclaiming, "I'm so drunk. Oh yes, I'm so drunk." He never hurt anyone, but his children were obviously embarrassed in front of their friends.

During the holidays, the celebration of the season began at school as we were instructed to use our blunt scissors to cut out turkey heads. The teacher proudly told the story again of "our" first Thanksgiving. Elementary school was a time in which we really did not know who we were or understand why we seemed to only be able to live in the Village and not within the neighborhood. The neighborhood children must have been equally as confused because they rarely even tried to venture into the Village for any occasion. In general, and on both sides, everybody seemed to be accepting and even content.

My mother-cousin diligently kept up with and tried to attend all the special programs scheduled for the holidays. There was usually at least one play with a seasonal theme given by the children. The roles of the heroic pilgrim characters usually were given to a Caucasian member of the student population. The school system for the most part didn't extend a great deal of encouragement to the children of the Village. Whatever motivation or special interest we developed, it could be credited either exclusively to: the positive influence of our parents or some other member of our extended Village family, or we were left to devise our own method to acquire success.

"Children, we're going to hold rehearsals for this year's play after school. I want to see the following students right after school today..." The teacher's announcement always started this way and at this point I tended to stop listening because I knew my name would not be mentioned.

One day, while rambling about on our property I wandered into an abandoned shed. Inside there were endless dusty boxes. After two days of rambling, I found an old violin. Somehow, I knew from the first moment I saw the instrument that it would become a part of my life. My mother and I rode the streetcar into the city and left the violin at a music shop to be refurbished.

The first day I proudly reported for orchestra practice I was in the third grade. I was given a book of scales and instructed to take a seat in the last chair of the violin section.

Willingly, I practiced the scales every evening after school for at least two hours. I even spent at least this much time trying to improve my skills on the weekends. I was infatuated by the delicate treasure and diligently began to spend hours tuning and cleaning it until the wood glistened.

The school usually took at least one field trip each year to see the Pittsburgh Symphony Orchestra perform. I was captivated and inspired by these concerts. The music was beautiful. I became convinced that with this glorious violin I could somehow work myself into the exclusive and elite group of peers that the teachers always seemed to hold in some special high esteem. I felt a deep sense of pride every day during my long walk to and from the bus stop with my instrument. I didn't mind having to struggle to balance my books while clinging tightly to the violin case with its broken handle.

Each year I waited and hoped to be recognized as qualified to be moved to a higher chair position in the orchestra. My parents and entire family continued to be amazed at my display of determination and dedication. The promotion became especially important to my progress with the instrument during the third year with the orchestra. Along with the obvious prestige the promotion would offer an opportunity to practice and be trained personally in private sessions after school by the orchestra leader. My parents couldn't afford private lessons. I knew that the only way to advance to a higher level with my beloved violin was to gain the promotion.

New members of the orchestra soon bypassed me, and I began to doubt my abilities. The peculiar thing was that the conductor never criticized my playing. I was now in sixth grade. At first, my only response was to practice longer and harder. I did this until my back and fingers ached. Still, the promotion did not happen and I began to realize that the conductor rarely even glanced in my direction. One day, before graduation from grade school, I approached my mother-cousin at the table in the kitchen and in a trembling voice asked, "What did I do wrong? I'm sorry if I failed you. I really tried and practiced. But, I guess I just wasn't good enough."

"Oh, you were good enough. Don't you ever doubt that, you hear me?" she answered with more than a bit of an edge in her voice. "You just don't understand. I hoped you wouldn't have to be disappointed like this. But down deep I was afraid it would turn out this way. I only wish I could afford to get you those private lessons."

By now I simply gave up fighting the tears and I crumbled into my mother's lap and began to cry. "I don't understand. What did I do?"

My mother never tried to answer the question. Instead, she just hugged me and rocked me back and forth. "It's going to be alright." This was all she kept repeating.

Perhaps the tears were my way of recognizing that a door had been closed for me. I knew that no matter how hard I tried to find a solution that there probably wasn't any way to overcome the missed opportunity.

"You were just as good, and maybe even better than lots of those other children," she said as she took my face between her hands and made me look directly in her eyes. "Now, you stop crying. Don't let anyone steal your dream. Just keep working because an education is the only thing nobody can take away from you. Keep playing that violin as best as you can."

The taste of disappointment remained deep in my heart even though I desperately tried to suppress it in front of my mother. Gradually, it was replaced by an even more determined attitude to somehow be recognized for my hard work in school. I now wanted to succeed despite the lack of support of a system that seemed to be willing to acknowledge only the achievements of my Caucasian peers.

Illustrated by Holly N. Avery 2012.

CHAPTER 12 -- CHRISTMAS AND BEER

Christmas was a time of stress for the children of the Village. It was confusing, to say the least. When we were very young, the Santa we visited downtown at Hornes and Gimbels department stores was of the same color as the people of the neighborhood. Our parents always insisted that we take the traditional annual photo with jolly ole Nick while posing on his knee. The pictures were then placed close to the Christmas tree and copies were sent to various relatives. These photos sometimes revealed one or more of us looking up in amazement and horror into Santa's face. If we resorted to crying, the pictures were referred to by our parents as, "cute, look at that sweet face."

I remember almost every session with Santa, especially those that occurred after my sixth birthday. At first, I was excited and I couldn't wait to tell him that all year I had been a good girl. Of course, he was supposed to know this. So, I was prepared to quickly move on to the list of toys I wanted for Christmas. I don't recall ever being afraid of him.

Yet, the simple trip to Santa's lap was soon about to take on another meaning as I approached my eighth birthday. By this time, I had observed many incidents of overt prejudice against black people by white people in almost every aspect of my life. As I waited in line for my turn to chat with Santa, I glanced from my mother's face, to the surrounding crowd and then I tried to look jovial Saint Nick directly in the eye. He didn't have to pick me up because I was now tall enough to easily slide myself onto his knee. However, it was necessary for him to support me with his hands on my forearms.

He quickly smiled at me, as he nodded his head towards the camera. This was an attempt by him to encourage me to smile. I put my head down and refused to look up. The fact was that I couldn't remember ever seeing a white person come to the Village for any good reason. It was beyond my capability to imagine that this white man would actually take it upon himself to come to your home just to deliver presents. The only time I recalled seeing white people in our small enclave was to collect insurance premiums or to repossess property.

The absence of many toys of color only added to our confusion. A coloring book that had drawings of real-life looking people presented a special challenge and often even frustration. Occasionally, I would consider coloring some of the heroic characters brown, but I never did. Consistently I made the choice to use the pink crayon for the skin and a light brown, red or yellow crayon for each and every character in my *Superman*, *Archie* and *Dick Tracy* coloring books. It simply didn't occur to me that people of my color did anything significant enough to qualify for inclusion in even a coloring book.

The neighborhood was lavishly decorated and the bells of their grand churches sounded Christmas carols. Each home seemed to have a huge tree, with tinsel and many sparkling lights. The windows themselves often had special messages written on them for their neighbors and the world to see. These encouraged "Peace on earth and good will to all men," "Noel," and "Silent night, holy night." The neighborhood children could be seen building snowmen in their front yards by the sides of their fathers. The men of the neighborhood usually worked until midday clearing the snow from the sidewalks in front of the festive houses.

A holiday celebration in the Village was always a time in which we traveled from home to home eating dinner after dinner at the insistence of our many self-appointed guardians. Adults of the Village accepted and relished their roles as parent to each and every child in the Village. Verbal reprimands were viewed as a community right of passage. These could be issued by any adult to any child at any time. We were told to respect our elders without any "backtalk." This dictate was the one line that was drawn in the sand by our parents that we did not dare cross.

An offense by a child of the Village merited immediate parental reports to every adult in the area. The adults would then work together to increase their careful observation of the offenders behavior for weeks or months. Distribution of an indisputable report of an offense was shared by the parents via telephone or if the offense warranted, delivered by the parent-guardian directly to the front door of the offender's home. The vigilance was performed not out of fear of harm from a stranger. They felt we required oversight to avoid "getting into trouble." We were annoyed and complained to each other for years about their vigilance. However, at this time of year we knew we were valuable and loved by our elders. It was especially comforting that these people who looked like us and spoke like us wanted only that we remain safe.

Many of our fathers had gotten lucrative jobs at the steel mills. It was an era of prosperity. It was also very much a time of community, sharing and warmth. We firmly believed the lives of the neighborhood children were just like what we saw on popular television shows of that era.

TV began at this time to be a very important shaper of our young minds. The only images on this new medium of colored men were few and far between. We watched the comedian Rochester on *The Jack Benny Show*, the painfully hilarious *Amos and Andy Show*, and Ray Charles whenever he made a special appearance on *The Ed Sullivan Show*.

I was a child who desperately searched for peace and tranquility. Perhaps this is why I adored Perry Como. In my eyes, he had a casual demeanor, effortless grace and reverence for all things large and small. It may be possible for me to credit the influence of Perry Como with my sometimes gullible belief that all white people are compassionate and caring people. Every time I watched his show I remember feeling that his world was truly a better place.

The Village feasted on dishes the parents had learned to prepare when they were children in the South. The homes of the Village had all been given a thorough holiday cleaning and the air surrounding the

Village smelled of turkey, chitterlings, sweet potato pie, sage, fresh baked rolls and ham. My need to escape decreased and it was replaced by a cautious sense of security.

The harmony of the Village generally suffered at least one major disruption due to the abundance of holiday alcohol. Substance dependency had long ago taken hold of some of the adults. It is certain that more than one of our parents would today be classified as a functioning alcoholic. We children learned the brand names of the daemons utilized by our parents to help to "make everything alright," "smooth out all the edges." I knew that alcohol was either brown or clear before I could write. Johnny Walker, Seagram's and Jack Daniels were all welcome in our home. Two cases of beer were purchased by the parents for every case of pop to be given to the children. It was only logical that the children would dedicate as much effort as necessary to the removal of as many bottles of beer as possible from the parental stashes.

One snowy evening, all the relatives assembled at our home and immediately the cases of Iron City Beer were hauled from the coal cellar to our kitchen. The tops began to pop.

I had devised a method to test the vigilance of the adults that consisted of simply walking around in the room where they sat to see if they noticed me. Experience had taught me that one of the few times an adult's ability to keep their children out of their business declined was after drinking too much. My first attempt nearly earned me a spanking.

"Girl, what are you doing here? Didn't we tell you to stay in your room?" This admonishment came from my mother as she made a vain effort to rise from her chair. I noticed towards the end of her statement she began to slur some of the words. Patiently, I went back upstairs to my room. I kept listening and waiting for my next opportunity.

The jazz and blues and smells of beer, bourbon, scotch and cigarette smoke filled the entire house. Occasionally, I could hear only bits and pieces of their conversations: "I told them that damn job wasn't no good. All them crackers want you to do is slave work." "I'm gonna hit that number, you know, the one I played last month and when I do, I'll be in New York or maybe back down home." "Damn that's some good scotch." "Listen to that beat. I saw that man break it down at a club in the Hill District." Their voices indicated that they were becoming more and more intoxicated. Soon, some of them stopped talking and began to sing along with the music.

I waited almost a half hour more just to be safe. Then I cautiously began to inch my way slowly down the creaking stairway. The plan seemed to be working. My mother had only been able to make her way to the kitchen to start trying to fry chicken. She was slumped forward with a cigarette still burning in her mouth. The raw chicken sat exposed on a sheet of waxed paper on top of the table. It hadn't even been cut up.

Usually, she was very careful not to spill a drop of flour. There was a collection of paper bags on top of the refrigerator that she used to dust the chicken with flour, salt and pepper. Before carefully placing floured chicken into the boiling hot grease, she always gave each piece an extra shake. Then, she would gently lower each piece into the bubbling Crisco. She only used expensive Crisco on the holidays. The rest of the year everything from bread to pork chops was fried or prepared using raw lard.

It was obvious that she had started to prepare the flour mixture. A trail of flour and grease was everywhere. Suddenly, she adjusted the cigarette hanging from her mouth and began to sing along with a Frank Sinatra hit on her favorite radio station, KDKA. Her back was turned to face the stove.

I knew it was impossible for her to see the cases of beer that sat in a corner. I stood to the side of the doorway of the living room at the foot of the steps. Only one more obstacle remained between me and my objective. I would have to cross in front of the doorway where the adults sat without being noticed.

As a whole, they all seemed to be in their own world. Some of them were still trying to hold conversations. For the most part, I realized they had all reached the point of being so drunk that it was not possible for them to notice much of any movement that was not directly in front of them. Quickly, I crossed the kitchen, removed three bottles of beer and managed to flee successfully back up the stairs.

Somehow, I removed the caps and quickly drank one bottle after the other. The only prior experience I had with the feeling of being dizzy was as a result of riding the merry-go-round. The alcohol began to take control. At first, it was a relaxing and enjoyable sensation. My room was always too cold. I noticed to my delight that a sweet and slow sensation of warmth surrounded me. Unfortunately, this was quickly replaced by an overpowering nausea. I began to gag and finally I threw up everything I had consumed for the past ten days.

I desperately tried to wipe up the vomit even as I continued to add more to the mess on my floor. I knew my actions and the evidence in front of me would surely cause me to get at least a severe spanking. Out of the corner of my blurred vision, I suddenly saw my mother standing directly over me. She grabbed my arm and stood me up to face her. "If you're grown enough to do this, you can clean it up. Go get the scrub bucket. I want this floor and your whole room spic and span. You understand me?"

All I could do was nod and lower my head to avoid seeing what I was sure would be the swing of her arm. I braced myself to receive the first of what could be hundreds of blows. I didn't know with what she planned to strike me. I just knew it was guaranteed to hurt.

Instead, she turned and left my room without another word. Immediately, I understood that I had to get myself out of this mess. The adults, that appeared to be in a collective coma when I went upstairs, had all suddenly come back to life. They pointed at me and laughed as I stumbled downstairs to retrieve the bucket of water and rags I would have to use to clean the room.

As I passed in front of the doorway to the living room I overheard my mother say, "Well, I rather she did this here kind of thing, right here at home. If she's gonna get into liquor, better that we're around to keep an eye on her." I was confused by these remarks when I started to be able to think clearly again. I felt that I deserved to be punished. It troubled me that she seemed to have almost expected this type of behavior from me. I struggled for many years to understand the mixed message. It occurred to me that her forgiving attitude was brought about because she saw something twisted in me that reminded her of my real mother.

After the holidays, the feelings of well-being and security for me and my Village peers quickly diminished. The world we returned to continued to be controlled by the neighborhood. It was becoming very apparent that some elements of the white neighborhood did not care in the least if we prospered. As we grew older, the manner in which we were treated, what we watched and how easily we were discounted provided us with countless reasons to flee the entire community.

CHAPTER 13 -- DEBBIE WAS DIFFERENT

Broken branches hit the side of the old house to mark the beginning of another cold and wet school day. The bedroom on the second floor had only one window. A constant and bitter draft from the space below the base of the window and along the border of the double panes was not tamed by the heat from the pot-bellied stove that seeped into the room via an open door from the living-room on the first floor. Breakfast aromas of coffee mixed with cigarettes indicated that the old stove had been fed a new supply of coal. There would be a pot of hot water waiting on top to be used for a morning face wash. Doors to all the other rooms on the second floor were closed in an attempt to send as much heat as possible into this one room. Often the air in the entire house remained barely warm enough to classify it as more comfortable inside than outside the dwelling.

Everything about our humble house was crooked. It was as if it had been built in great haste and without the advantages of a level. The walls had been painted, then papered then painted again directly over the paper in some places. Soot from the pot-bellied stove had seeped into almost everything. Nothing in the house was new. The floor creaked whenever, and wherever I walked.

I crawled out from underneath the warm quilt and double-blanket combination and lowered my feet into my sling-back house shoes that sat on the frigid, wooden floor. The first mission was to bundle-up enough to make a quick run to the outside toilet. I returned from the trip around the side of the house and down a short path to the bathroom thoroughly and rudely awaken by the wind that now had taken advantage of its opportunity to reach every inch my body.

Complete and thorough personal hygiene had to be addressed in the evenings when for a few hours the house seemed warm. Only a hasty cleansing of the face and hands and brushing of teeth could be accomplished in the morning while standing next to the pot-bellied stove.

My father had been home from work for a couple hours. It was his job every morning to make sure I got off to school on time. This job was assigned to him since my mother always left for work before six in order to prepare breakfast for her rich, German employer.

"You're gonna' have to hurry or you'll miss the bus. There's some oatmeal in the pot, if you want it. Don't forget that after school your Mama wants you to stop by her job," he reminded me from the kitchen. Every morning he said about the same thing. Like most eleven year olds, I probably really absorbed only a small portion of his announcement.

I finished dressing and made an extra effort to thoroughly dry my hands in order to protect them from the bitterly cold temperatures I'd encounter during the two mile walk to the bus stop. After dressing, I went to the kitchen and peeked into the pot on top of the stove. It contained the oatmeal my father always prepared for our breakfast.

"No thanks Daddy, I'm not hungry," was the standard response I usually gave him as I kissed him on the cheek and headed towards the door. The comforting morning's traditional and quiet routine with my father ended when I opened the crooked front door and headed across the yard. After climbing up the slippery steps to the road that ran above the gully, I continued fighting the wind head-on and finally reached the base of the Village.

The divisive hedge marked the midpoint of my walk to the bus stop. By the time I arrived there, I had already started to feel chilled to the bone. The heavy coat I wore barely reached the hemline of my dress. The wind used this as it would a tunnel to run its course from that point up to my calf. My shoes were so wet that I had the impression that I was walking barefooted. Knee socks, with an inherent tendency to creep down your legs slowly, and a skull cap offered little protection in reality from either cold or blowing rain.

Another mile of walking through the neighborhood with the wind in my face still had to be conquered. Usually, once I reached the divisive hedge, I would join as many as ten other children of the Village to complete the walk to the bus stop. Our group often contained at least one representative from all the families. I was grateful in a way for the foul weather. The lazy bullies and teasers were so miserable that they did not have the presence of mind to single out any poor victim for torture. Once at the bus stop, I alternated from one foot to the other and tried to find shelter behind a telephone pole from the piercing wind. The few kids from the neighborhood that shared the stop with us stood huddled together. The two groups of children rarely greeted one another. It was extremely unusual for a conversation to take place even though they lived well within a block of each other.

The bus stop was in front of a small privately owned grocery store. Most mornings it was closed. After school, we were delighted to see their Coca Cola sign hung on the door indicating they were now open They were eager to sell the children Wise potato chips, Hostess Twinkies and numerous other snacks. The primary items that the small neighborhood market specialized in were cigarettes, bread and lunchmeat of various kinds. It never offered a large selection. In order to do any serious grocery shopping, a walk of an additional two miles was required to reach the local A&P.

I was grateful to get on the bus simply because it was heated. The unthawing would have been a good thing if it had not marked the beginning of taunting and heckling from the bullies. The bus was full almost to its capacity of perhaps 40 children. Sitting in the long back seat was the most prized position and it was always occupied by the older kids from the neighborhood. Generally, if there was a seat available it was taken strictly according to the community pecking order.

This morning I stood in my normal position in the aisle midway to the back of the bus. I talked to my friends from the Village about completed and incomplete homework. Sometimes, we also talked about the latest movies our parents had taken us to see in downtown Pittsburgh. On Fridays, the topic was always what we planned to do for the weekend. It never dawned on me to conduct this same conversation with one of the neighborhood kids. The most I had to say to them was usually, "Excuse me," as I got on or off the bus. Everything seemed normal that particular day, until I felt a tap on my shoulder.

A white girl who stood beside me suddenly said, "Hi, my name is Debbie and this is my first day at school. I'm from New York and we just moved here." I looked at her in confusion. I thought to myself that she surely wasn't talking to me. But, to my amazement she continued, "Boy it sure is cold today."

All I could muster was a "huh huh." I believed this stupid and curt response would end the whole thing. Instead, she continued to talk on and on about how excited she was to be living in Pittsburgh. I didn't say another word to her. I even turned my head to avoid looking at her. The bus continued to twist and turn its way along the four mile ride to school. Debbie never seemed to take a breath between words.

When I got off the bus a few of my friends of the Village poked me in the side and whispered questions in an attempt to assess the situation. "Who was she?" "What did she want?"

The only answer I could come-up with was something like, "I don't know."

Debbie found me again later that day in the cafeteria. I remember feeling embarrassed to be the subject of this strange white girl's attention. Didn't she know the rules? I felt like every eye in the lunchroom was fixed right on me. But, Debbie was determined. She followed me to a table and put her tray down with mine without an invitation.

I don't recall again the subjects that she discussed. I do remember the expressions of shock on the faces of both the children of the Village and those of the neighborhood. My Village friends usually joined me for lunch. Instead, they found another table and became a part of the throng of eyes that were now fixed in my direction. Debbie jumped right into her lunch and ceaseless conversation.

Out of the corner of my eye I noticed a few of the neighborhood girls gather near the entrance to the cafeteria. One of them pointed and the others appeared to be as embarrassed as I was regarding Debbie's behavior. I hardly ate more than a few bites. Debbie chatted on and on. Suddenly the pressure and my personal embarrassment were too much. I stood up and made some lame excuse to leave the table. Unable to return to class and not willing to face my friends at the other table, I headed for the only door in order to exit the cafeteria.

One of the neighborhood girls lunged forward and got right in my face to say, "Who do you think you are nigger." I had escaped years of confusion and confrontation at this school by sticking to a simple rule. The rule was, "Don't screw with the system." Now the system demanded an accounting and I didn't have a clue what to say in my defense. Not on just one, but two occasions I had been observed being friendly with one of them and they knew that I knew that I'd stepped over the line.

The bell rang indicating it was time to return to class. At least for a while, it allowed me to escape persecution.

Debbie and I weren't in the same grade so I didn't see her again until after school on the bus. This time, she was more reserved and didn't even try to strike-up a conversation. My friends from the Village asked me the same questions they had that morning. Never once during the long ride home did Debbie approach me. Instead she seemed content now to carry on conversations with the older neighborhood girls. I didn't know if she was tired of trying to force herself on me or if someone from the neighborhood had explained the system to her. Knowing that I had another year to continue to ride on the bus, I was just glad the whole thing was over.

CHAPTER 14 -- THE SHOE STORE

Practically all the people living within a four mile radius of the Village were of European descent. They were either first or second generation Americans. The Germans and Jews seemed to own or manage the majority of the local businesses. This was especially true of those that sold appliances, cars and clothing. All the really good restaurants and delis were in the hands of the Italians. The ethnic group at the very bottom of the pile that earned the least money and did not own much of anything could trace their roots to Poland. The accepted dislike for the black Village population became more intense as you moved down the neighborhood's white social ladder.

A twisted "caring practice" was adhered to by some adult members of the neighborhood to keep the Village in its proper social position. It strongly resembled the sick paternal-caring system that had been successfully utilized by the more clandestine white Klan supporters in the South. If asked, it was highly likely that a neighborhood member would state firmly that as far as he was concerned there were no problems with the Negroes in the Village. After all, they had good jobs now and their kids were allowed to attend the same schools as his kids. He understood his position. He would probably admit that he did "keep an eye" on "them coloreds" if quarried for greater detail. The justification we generally heard for the application of the caring practice was that they watched us for our own protection. It was all done, "just in case something happened."

The "caring practice" was simple to apply and it did not require much maintenance. A dignified nod of the head for senior members of the Village was the common greeting they used while passing an adult of the Village on the street. It used to irritate me when they referred to my father as "James." Most of the time, they boldly used the first name of our parents even though they weren't our friends. This did not happen in the Village. There, my father was always, Mr. Washington. The caring practice permitted them to behave towards us as if we were less than them.

They expected our parents to keep us in line. My peers and I were repeatedly warned to behave ourselves in their presence. We were also told to always address any adult as Mr. or Miss. The only time any resident of the Village seemed to have value was when we were able to afford to shop in their specialty stores.

On one occasion, my mother took me to an exclusive shoe store in the neighborhood to buy a pair of black boots I'd seen in their front display window. She and I both realized, without saying anything to each other, that the clerk for the most part was ignoring us. People in those days were overly courteous. I wouldn't dare grab the display model or even attempt to sit down on the bench for measurement without an invitation. We continued to stand without as much as a polite acknowledgement from the clerk. Finally, she reluctantly turned her attention to us. She did this small acknowledgement only after she had waited on two other customers who had entered the store after us. The ill-tempered women huffed and sighed as she tried to force herself to talk to us. She continued to stare into the cash register drawer rather look at us. Finally, she firmly folded her arms defiantly in front of her pointed bra covered chest, signed heavily and said, "Well now, may I help you?"

The woman wore a great deal of makeup. The arch of her eyebrows had been enhanced to the point that they looked like they were at least two inches above her eye sockets. Every time she addressed my mother she had a tendency to arch her left eyebrow even further. This caused the left side of her mouth to also twist upward as if she had smelled something really horrible.

"My daughter was interested in trying on those black shoes over there." My mother nodded her head in the direction of the displays along the side of the wall and added, "The ones with the high sides going up your ankle." She considered it improper and uncouth to point her finger for any reason.

"Those are our latest arrivals. They are not on sale. Are you sure you want to see that model?" There was no question in my mind that she asked this stupid question in order to further insult us. Before we could reply, the bell above the front door rang announcing the arrival of a new customer. She suddenly put her hands on her hips and began to move towards the recent arrival. I knew that this was her way to further display and emphasize her disdain for us.

"Yes, that's what I want to see." My mother and I had already begun to move towards the bench to try on the shoes. Unfortunately, politeness demanded that we had to continue standing awkwardly over the bench until we were given some sort of gesture or statement from the clerk to sit down.

By now, she seemed to have completely abandoned us. As a courtesy to the tall Caucasian man that was her new customer, she approached him smiling and said, "Good afternoon sir. I'll be right with you."

At this point, she reluctantly returned her attention back to us. "What size will that be?" The blatant chill in her voice let us know beyond a doubt that she was thoroughly disgusted.

We usually bought shoes downtown. In those stores I was just another customer. I was accustomed to having my foot measured before trying on a new pair of shoes. "I think we need a size seven and a half." indicated my mother.

"Alright, just a minute." She darted by us towards the back of the store and several minutes later returned with a box and handed them to me. "Will that be all?"

"Just a minute. Honey, sit down and try them on." My mother's response clearly aggravated the clerk who crossed her arms in front of her and sighed loudly to further demonstrate her irritation.

I took the shoes out of the box and tried them on. They seemed to fit exactly like I imagined they would. "They're fine Mama."

"We'll take them then." She smiled at me and hugged me gently on the forearm. As she gingerly rose from the bench beside me, she laughed and complained about her favorite subject, arthritis. "One day, I swear, these ole legs are gonna improve. I'm stiff as a board." Once on her feet, she started searching her purse for her wallet and slowly walked towards the counter.

I gave the box back to the clerk who hurriedly pushed it into a bag. At the register she forced herself to begin to complete our transaction. Again, with her eyebrow over-arched, she held her hand out to demand payment. "That will be $22."

We paid for the shoes and without another word started to depart the store. As we passed the new customer we heard the clerk say to him, "Well now Sir, now what can I get for you?"

"Nothing. I don't think I want to shop here anymore." At this point he turned his back to the clerk and managed to reach the exit door before us. A kind and warm smile covered his face as he looked into my mother's eyes and said, "Let me get the door for you."

I hadn't seen this man before and even though I always looked for him as long as I lived in the Village, I never saw him again. He was one of many white people in the neighborhood who seemed to understand and sympathize with our plight. Some extended credit so that we could always buy food or receive dental and medical treatment. Others would smile at us as we walked through the neighborhood for no reason. Unfortunately, they were not in the majority.

"I took the shoes out of the box and tried them on. They seemed to fit exactly like I imagined they would." Illustrated by Deanna Graves 2012.

CHAPTER 15 -- GOSSIP AND RELATED CONFUSION

One thing always remained constant in our household. My mother was wise enough to doubt the observations of her neighbors. She openly bragged about this lack of trust and advised me to follow in her footsteps. The reason she gave was simple, "to avoid confusion."

I believe that she hated confusion worst than she professed to hate Satan himself. She liked to say, "There ain't no way to lock out Satan. But nobody will bring confusion in my house." Her efforts to bar Satan and gain some sort of orderly thought were futile. Both Satan and confusion often reigned in our home.

She spent any spare time she could arrange sitting in the kitchen at a wooden table that constantly wobbled. There, she drank from a cup of Maxwell House coffee while chain-smoking Pall Mall cigarettes. In front of her, and on the floor beside her, there would be magazines and newspapers from which she diligently conducted searches to find interesting recipes.

We had an old wood-burning stove for many years that required constant attention. One day, she somehow acquired a brand-new electric range. I wasn't sure which store sold us the appliance. I was positive though that it was another credit purchase. I never felt comfortable using things purchased on credit. Every time I used or wore them, I kept waiting for someone to come and take them back.

A gleaming assortment of pots and pans were soon purchased. The reason for buying them was given by my mother as, "Those ole pots and pans just ain't gonna do the trick anymore. When I want to use the oven to bake, I don't want no pan to be the reason my cakes don't rise."

The front door of the house opened directly into the kitchen. The first thing she tried to do after coming home from work was to kick off her shoes and spend at least a few minutes in her treasured new kitchen gathering her thoughts before she started to prepare dinner. Many times my father and I had been warned in no uncertain terms that she felt she deserved this time in which she would not tolerate any confusion.

The wooded and hilly area that separated our house from the main street of the Village was often used by sexually active Village children to culminate their illusions. The urge to belong to and be a part of someone else started to increase in power until it was common for a few of the Village girls at the invitation of the always eager Village boys to begin to agree to frequent the wooded refuge. I was aware of the meetings and had overheard and seen some of the encounters. I continued to refuse the persistent invitations of the sexually curious and overly motivated young men. My mother's cache of horrifying tales of the life of her prodigal daughter had already begun to cause me to reject dangerous situations. Images in my head of her crawling through the streets in search of the next man and another drink filled me with fear. At this time, the very thought of her twisted lifestyle made it easy for me to repress any interest I might have in the mystery of sexual satisfaction.

One late afternoon, during the summer of my eleventh year, I had come home with the hope of enjoying the latest edition of Ebony magazine. I really liked reading the huge new editions while listening to the deep, resonating voice of the sexy evening shift disc jockey on R&B radio station, WAMO. My mother did not know that I was home. She'd just gotten off from work and barely had time to get inside the house when there was a knock on the door. I peeked out the upstairs window and saw one of our neighbors chatting with my mother. Every once in a while the neighbor would stop and point towards the woods. Unfortunately, I was too far away to hear clearly. No matter how hard I tried to listen I never heard one word of the conversation.

I did realize though that this was probably very serious simply because we rarely had uninvited company. There were two very good reasons for what appeared to be a lack of hospitality on our part. My parents were seldom home during the day because they worked. Added to this was the fact that our twisted, dangerous stairway was located at the bottom of a gully. It required a great deal of effort just to reach our front door. I didn't know what type of news the neighbor had brought, but I did sense that it was definitely not good news.

I gave up trying to overhear the conversation. In just a few minutes, I was relieved when I heard our screen door snap shut. The next sound from the kitchen was that of rattling pots and pans. I relaxed because I was sure that my mother would not be simply settling into cooking dinner if the news had been "confusing."

Suddenly, the phone began to ring. After only a few minutes, I overheard my mother say, "I don't know who that heifer is, but it ain't my daughter."

At this point, I didn't know what I should do next. The worst situation for a child to be in is not to know exactly if they are or are not in trouble. If I was in trouble, would it be better to face it now? If I was in trouble, shouldn't I remember whatever it was that I had done wrong? I replayed the entire day in my mind retracing every step I'd taken and couldn't recall an infraction. So, I decided to simply face the unknown and its possible related punishment. I turned off the radio and bravely walked down the stairs to face what could be a blistering situation.

"Hi Momma." This was all I could muster as I descended the stairwell. She looked up at me and nodded. Suddenly, I thought of something else to say that would make it appear things were normal. I added, "What's for dinner?" I prayed that she'd view this as a benign question. By then I had reached the front of the stove. In a further attempt to fake a light-hearted, normal day attitude, I peeked underneath the top of a pot of water that had just begun to boil.
She walked toward me and looked me in the face and warmly smiled. "I was thinkin' hamburgers and macaroni and cheese. Are you hungry?"

I wanted to say, "Not as hungry as I am relieved." Instead, I just smiled at her and walked towards the steps. The phone began to ring again. She had left it on the side of the table at the bottom of the steps. As she crossed the kitchen under her breath I heard her complain that with so many calls she'd never finish preparing dinner and get any rest.

This time after a quick hello she stood in the middle of the floor with the phone in one hand and her trusty Pall Mall in the other listening intently to the conversation on the other end of the line. "Hold on a minute." she asked the caller and with the hand holding the cigarette she motioned for me to go upstairs.

Immediately, and without any questions I did exactly as I was told. Curiosity prevented me from going any further than the top of the steps. From there, I heard the rest of the conversation. My mother informed the caller, "You're the third damn person to bother me with this shit and I'll only tell you that whoever's in the woods ain't my daughter."

Now, I was able to put two and two together. I knew exactly what had happened. I felt very special at that moment because this was the point in our relationship when we managed to turn together in a very positive direction. I was especially grateful that she had defended me, and amazed that she'd done this without knowing exactly where I was at the time the incident occurred.

To be honest, I did know exactly who was in the woods that day. There was only one girl in the Village that was about the same size and shape as me. I don't have any doubt that my mother must have also realized exactly who she was and what she was doing alone in the woods with a boy. The true guilty party was the daughter of one of my mother's oldest friends. To my knowledge, my mother never in any way confronted her friend with this hurtful information.

Her noble behavior proved two very important life lessons for me. The first was that if you don't have anything good to say, you shouldn't say anything at all. The second was to beware of a dog carrying a bone. These two logical guidelines have prevented me from losing friends and placing undeserved value on hurtful information.

This was the one time that my mother won her battle against her two most formidable enemies. At least on this day, Satan did not gain entry into our home and confusion was kept away from our door.

CHAPTER 16 -- TAXES AND OTHER NUMBERS

The dark and rich volcanic soil that surrounded the house in the gully was moist beyond belief. My mother was fond of savoring the smell while holding it in her hand. She would then compress then decompress the soil to demonstrate how well it still held together. The land and the old green and gray frame house were her prized possessions.

During those days, the true enemy of the people of the Village was the "tax man." Constant hard and demeaning work for unappreciative employers had to be performed by my parents to avoid missing even one payment on a tax lien they had accumulated long ago to pay for the education of their only natural daughter. My mother had a reputation for compassion, fearlessness and personal strength. It was important to her to "Render unto Caesar that which is Caesar's." Therefore, the debt was never denied. It literally hung over the house in the gully like an axe.

In addition to the tax lien, both of my parent-cousins were very fond of the finer things life had to offer. The closets in the broken-down house contained lavish clothing including an ermine coat. The "Sunday-funeral" clothes I wore were mostly purchased on-time. Somehow, my mother managed to obtain credit cards at all the best stores in Pittsburgh. Money and the acquisition of money demanded that she find an extra means of support. As a result my mother began a long financial relationship with a branch of a racketeering Jewish family. She soon established a way for the Village adults to play the numbers without leaving the comforts of their own homes.

Playing the numbers was illegal and can be compared to participating in a lottery. The idea is to get the right combination of a series of three numbers. This was considered a "hit." There were different levels of "hits," and it was possible to play a long-shot and "hit" at even a thousand-to-one. Often I was given the responsibility to carry the "slips." The "slips" were pieces of paper on which a Village member listed his numbers along with his wager of the day.

I began to carry numbers for my mother around the age of 8 or 9. The adults frequently asked me what number I thought would be a sure winner. At first, I provided them whatever figure came into my head. Frequently, the numbers I gave them actually hit. They often rewarded me with up to a dollar when I dropped by to pay them cash in a small paper bag for their hit.

It didn't take long to realize that I could make a little money for myself on the side. I approached one of my mother's regular customers and told him that I would share my favorite number with him if he agreed to share his winnings with me when it hit. He was aware of my luck with the numbers. While kidding me and chastising me at the same time for, "actin' too damn grown," he quickly agreed. The number I gave him was, 477. That number or a combination of that number hit at least four times over the next year. I don't know if my mother knew about this racket I had on the side. If she did she never mentioned it.

Soon I realized that if I provided numbers to some of the other customers, my odds of winning would also increase. So, I casually struck more deals. In order to keep track, I started to jot down the numbers I recommended and to whom they were given. The return on this strategy was tremendous. In a short time, I saw a revenue increase. I quickly and easily became an 11 year old hustler. Because I lived in a household that was supported by the revenue from the numbers, it never occurred to me that this behavior was in any way abnormal.

The police for some reason did not even seem to care. If they were being paid under the table the money probably came from further up the feeding chain. The income from the numbers assured us there would be food on the table and helped to pay those never-ending and sometimes increasing bills.

The ever-present tax lien payments and mounting installment debt was not appeased by the additional income from the numbers. It is possible that my parents were really greedy and perhaps even bad managers of their resources. The bottom-line was that there was never enough money. Often, one of my parents "hit" the numbers. The joy was short-lived because they immediately had to spend that money to pay bills.

What funds the bill collectors didn't get too often found its way into the greedy hands of some supposedly needy relative. These leaches would crawl out of the woodwork and suddenly appear at our door before the money from the "hit" was in the hands of my mother. Instead of enjoying a better standard of living, the pressure to pay kept mounting. The health of my parents was finally destroyed by the crushing weight imposed by these oppressive obligations.

My childhood was filled with drama and contradictions. The only way I knew to deal with life was to meet it head on. I struggled to grow-up to become both an agile hustler and a good Christian. I was filled with guilt each time the Sunday school teacher told the story of how Christ threw the gamblers out of the temple. On the other hand, after church I was proud to stand in front of the counter at the ice cream parlor and order any old thing that crossed my mind.

I was now wearing a better and more comfortable pair of shoes. The quality of my dresses had also greatly improved. My winter coat was brand new, and I was able to buy a new beige, light-weight jacket to wear during the spring and summer. At home after church every Sunday, I was now delighted to be able to enjoy a decent cut of meat. Prior to the influx of cash from the numbers, we were only able to eat meat a few times each month. Fried chicken or round steak was served on these infrequent occasions. Our staples, before the numbers, were the all-too-familiar neck-bones and white navy beans.

My mother's life had begun in the deep woods of North Carolina. She was born shortly after the turn of the 20th century. Her family migrated to Pittsburgh before her eighth birthday. At first, her parents established themselves in a neighborhood in the inner city of Pittsburgh. A favorite story she used to love to tell was of a confrontation she had when she was not yet ten. A white boy made the mistake of calling her a nigger. According to her, he had barely uttered the hated word before she took a stick to him. She liked to conclude the story by assuring anyone listening that she was still a formidable foe. I knew what she was saying was true. Not even one adult in the Village ever dared to confront her.

The stick she used against the white boy had been long replaced by a .357 magnum. The instruction given to me regarding this weapon was, "Never pull it out unless you intend to use it." I found out much later that it is a rule followed by those that know how to survive in the streets. My mother was preparing me for life beyond the Village. She hoped that because of these harsh lessons, I would be able to survive no matter what type of lifestyle I eventually chose for myself.

She was also valued by members of the Village who knew she had the capacity to be warm and compassionate. It was easy for this woman, who was uneducated yet obviously extremely intelligent, to encourage me to play a violin and to do well in school. She had a deep love for classical music and a commitment to education. Whenever a problem existed that seemed insurmountable, it was not uncommon for Village members to make their way to our door to seek her guidance.

This was especially true for members of our family who would fall on hard times. She displayed towards them a genuine, kind and generous spirit. This often meant supplying food and clothing to both the parents and their children. When they first came to our door, my mother always advised them that their stay should be a short one. They were also warned that while they resided under her roof, they had to abide by her rules. Most of them understood that this was a temporary situation and their stays with us were often enjoyable. However, others tried to abuse her good natured assistance. The ungrateful relatives would soon find their few boxes of clothing and personal possessions sitting outside the house. On these occasions, there never were any disagreements or discussions. Everyone knew that when my mother had enough of a situation it was futile and even dangerous to dare to confront her.

The only thing that never ran away from my mother was debt.

CHAPTER 17 -- A CHILD IS A BLESSING

Household tasks never held my interest. Instead I was the shadow that tried to follow every step taken by my father. When he repaired the always-broken thirty or some stairs that ran down the hill of the gully to the house, I was the one who handed him the nails. If he was in the creek beneath the bridge to add rocks to the supports, I was right there beside him. I preferred the company of this quiet and strong little man who never complained and seemed to hold everything inside. The only time I was not allowed to follow him was when he ventured to the Village watering hole. This gentle man became the standard by which I have measured boyfriends, lovers and husbands. I never doubted that he loved me even though I was not his flesh and blood child.

The one memory which I can never erase from my mind is in reference to how my father broke me from being pigeon-toed. Perhaps the tendency to walk while pointing my toes inward had resulted from the abuse I had suffered as a baby. My mother repeatedly asked our family physician if he thought I should have braces. The doctor indicated that I would probably grow out of what he considered to be only a bad habit. I also sucked my thumb with a passion so she accepted his theory. On the other hand, my father would have no part of the notion. One day, he single-handedly solved both bad habits.

Early one bright and sunny morning, I hurried to get out of bed. I was an excited six year old who couldn't wait to dress and join my father for our weekly trip to the hardware store. He fixed us a small breakfast and then we walked across the yard, up the wooden steps in the gully and onto the street above the house. I usually skipped along in front of him. This time he took me by the hand and said, "Let me see you walk." I walked a few steps ahead of him and stopped. "Now, walk back to me." He paused a few seconds and added, "Oh, no. That won't do."

I didn't understand what he was talking about until he explained that in order to continue go to the store with him I would have to stop walking pigeon-toed. Then he calmly added, "And, you're going to have to give up that thumb sucking thing too."

After we returned from the store he immediately found my mother and said, "I want you to look at this." He pointed to me and indicated that he wanted me to walk. I admit to struggling but proudly put down one foot after the other with toes pointed forward. It took a bit longer to break the thumb habit. With his insistence it too became an embarrassing part of my history a few days before my seventh birthday.
One of his favorite things was to carry my bike up the dangerous gully steps for me. He always told me that

he did this because he didn't want me to hurt myself. He contracted bone cancer before my eleventh birthday. This form of cancer is a slow and malicious killer. In his case, over the period of two years, it robbed him of the ability to do much more than sit in a chair for hours. While he was still able to walk around, he desperately tried to do all his regular chores.

No matter how much I protested, he still insisted on carrying my bike up the long series of wooden steps. On what was to become one of the saddest day of my life, I argued with him and literally begged him not to try to carry it. He insisted and snatched the bike from my grasp. I continued to stand there motionless because I didn't know if I should try to help him by supporting it in the rear or just continue to do nothing. He had hardly taken more than five steps before I could see the pain overcome his body. I watched him crumble and fall into the weeds beside the stairway. I ran to his side and helped him crawl to the stairwell. Once there he said, "Now, I'm ok. You just go on. Daddy can't carry it for you no more." He always carried a huge handkerchief he liked to call his sweat rag in the back pocket of his overhauls. His hands were shacking, but he managed to pull out the rag.

"Daddy, I can't leave you. Let me go get somebody. Please." I continued to beg while I helped him to sit down to the side of one of the lower steps.

"No. Don't worry nobody. Just you get along. I'll sit here and catch my breath." In those days, you did as you were told. I stopped trying to persuade him. Instead, I stepped back from him and quickly retrieved the bicycle. As I approached the steps with the bike, I heard him struggle to resist one of what were now frequent coughing attacks.

Soon, the intense sorrow I felt in my throat seemed to expand into my chest. I was nearly overcome by the need to cry. All I wanted to do was to sit down beside him and comfort him like he had done for me so many times. But crying was not an option. My father had always wanted me to see him as a strong and capable man. I realized that he would interpret my tears as a form of pity.

The only thing I could do to get rid of intense sorrow that had now reached into my chest was to allow myself to cry. I obeyed him and struggled with the awkward weight of the bike to climb the stairs. In vain, I did all I could to resist looking back at my father. I wanted to scream for someone to help him. But I knew this would only make him angry. The further from him that I got, the less control I maintained over my emotions. The tears were freely flowing down my cheeks when I finally reached the road above the crooked house in the gully. I couldn't even see the gravel beneath my feet through the tears. My hands were trembling and my heart felt like it was in my throat. I knew I would not be able to convince him to accept help. I also realized it was important to him that I leave. There was absolutely nothing I could do. I kept looking back at him to make sure he hadn't fallen again. I continued to watch him until his image was hidden by the trees and bushes. When I thought that he couldn't see me any longer, I stopped and allowed myself to weep.

The ruler of our home was unquestionably my mother. She administered punishment with a twinkle in her eye. It was not uncommon for her to add to my grief by demanding that I go outside and pick the switch from the tree to be used by her to blister my behind. There weren't any social organizations established in those days to prevent parents from spanking a child in the middle of downtown Pittsburgh right in front of the Public Safety Building. On the other hand, parents rarely tried to intentionally manhandle or murder their children as is a popular and despicable practice today. Children were considered a blessing by the majority. If abuse existed, it was quickly dealt with by some member of the child's extended family. My mother did not spare the rod even though she often spoiled her children.

When I was in the fourth grade, a white boy who sat next to me continued to talk after the teacher issued a warning for us all to be quiet. He was not deterred by her general admonishment. Instead, his snickering grew even louder. At this point, the teacher rose from her desk. As she began to walk down the aisles, she suddenly called out my name. I immediately responded, "Yes, ma'am." I hadn't said a word and I wondered why she had decided to pick my name to emphasize her point with the class. She returned to her desk only after throwing a threatening look in my direction.

Unfortunately, the noise did not abate. In response, this time she began to charge down the aisle with a ruler in her hand. The next thing I knew she was right over my desk. The ruler was cocked back above her head and I knew she was going to punish someone. That someone turned out to be me. Before I could try to protect myself, she struck me in the right corner of my upper lip. The metal edge protector of the ruler grazed my mouth and blood started to run down my chin. Teachers also had more latitude to punish in those days. They could even employ a form called "corporal punishment" that allowed them to use vented paddles. I was sent to the nurse. After being dismissed early, I cried all the way home.

Deep down in my heart I was afraid that I would surely be sent to the yard to fetch a switch. I was confident that my mother would believe I had been disrespectful to the teacher causing this woman to have to resort to issuing a well-deserved piece of personal punishment.

I found her washing greens in the kitchen. When she saw my face, she immediately stopped what she was doing, grabbed me by my arm and pulled me closer to her so that she could get a better look. "What happened to you girl?" she asked.

Half crying and with tears flowing beyond control, I told her the story. To my amazement, she remained calm while she wiped her hands. Her next move frightened me. It was then that she went upstairs and grabbed the .357 magnum and her purse. The next thing I knew she took me by the hand and we were sitting on the trolley on our way to my school.

My mother walked into my classroom and confronted the pale and obviously terrified teacher. She quietly warned her that it would not be advisable for her to ever again think about hitting her daughter. The other teachers and the principal wisely kept their distance. Not one of them dared to approach her. They recognized that she was a woman who was beside herself with anger. She never took the weapon out of her purse that day. Instead, she held the imposing well-educated white people at bay with the strength of her commitment and more than a few choice curse words.

I was shocked to find out that my mother actually understood that it was possible for some elementary school teachers to be either a blessing or a curse.

The .357 magnum was a blue-plate policeman special and there would be many more times that it was used as a threat without being seen. However, the day did arrive when overcome by grief, she would actually use it.

CHAPTER 18 -- THE PECULIAR OLDER SISTER

The prodigal daughter of my parent's youth infrequently returned. When she did find her way back to their home, she was usually dragging along one of her many common-law husbands. The blurred reality she found in life was located at the bottom of a liquor bottle. Her IQ was tested and determined to be extremely high. The entire Village was excited when she headed off to Tuskegee Institute in Alabama to acquire the first degree in the family. Everyone held high hopes for her success.

Ironically, during her lifetime she never held a job that utilized or expanded the documented intellectual ability. She was a dark and beautiful woman with high cheekbones. Despite being intoxicated most of the time, she possessed a love of the finer foods, makeup and very expensive clothing. Her husbands and lovers tended to usually work as mechanics or gamblers.

Those fortunate enough to strike her interest sometimes had to shamelessly hustle on the side by gambling. All of them had one thing in common, a job. She wouldn't have anything to do with a man who wouldn't work for a living. They freely gave her every cent of their wages. Her beauty and free-loving reputation preceded her. The men clamored after her. It was not an uncommon occurrence for them to shamelessly fight each other for the privilege of being the one that could give her whatever she wanted. Their foolish generosity and desire to please her seemed to always lead to an eviction. She was very particular about where she lived. The result was that the apartments she chose were usually very expensive. When the rent could not be paid, she always knew her parents would accept and protect her. In the middle of the night she would appear at the door and begin to involve us in her living hell.

My parents' other daughter became the first person I knew that fiercely "bit the hand that fed her." It was necessary for me to tip around the house to avoid disturbing her once she stumbled off to sleep. Every evening began for her with a drink. The one drink lead to several others. We all knew she was a functioning alcoholic. Amazingly, she seemed to always manage to sober up enough to report to the local hospital where she held a full-time job on the evening shift as a nurse's aide.

Our house was always hopelessly cluttered, but we were forced to make room for her boxes of clothing, shoes, cosmetics and purses. At some point her wants and needs simply took over the entire household. She never had a child but always maintained some kind of pet. The poor cat, dog or bird generally remained behind with us once she and her husband (or lover) were able to find another willing landlord.

Her level of consumption of alcohol by the fifth-sized bottle was unbelievable. She seemed to have an equally insatiable thirst for trouble and confusion. Under the influence she would say anything to her parents. They remained determined and repeatedly tried to convince her that they only wanted to help her. For some reason beyond my ability to fathom, my mother suffered many bouts of verbal abuse from her other daughter without much protest. Instead, she usually launched into a long prayer session and increased her attendance at church. I overheard the prayers and witnessed her pleading with the Lord for a solution to her daughter's many disgraceful problems.

At times, it was necessary for my parents, aunt, cousins and uncle, to travel in the middle of the night to the inner city to rescue her from numerous life-threatening situations. There was one occasion when the grown-ups were forced to take my cousin and I along because they couldn't find anyone to watch us at three in the morning. We found her in a booth in a Chinese restaurant being held around the throat by one of her outraged common-law husbands. When she saw us she shouted, "All of you can kiss my ass." She continued to verbally lash out at our family even as my father pulled her from the grasp of a man who seemed determined to kill her. The common-law husband realized he was surrounded and did not dare to move a muscle.

Upon being released, she tried to stand upright. It was at this time that I noticed she was covered in vomit. Instead of being grateful for being saved from what could have been a certain death, she ran from table to table grabbing soy sauce bottles, utensils and napkin holders and hurled them in the direction of my mother. Profanity and evil threats kept coming from her mouth as my uncle, father and cousin struggled to capture her. Finally, they were able to pin her to the floor. She left the building being dragged by all but one leg that she managed to free from their grasps.

Somehow the family got her back to the Village and into bed. I watched my mother in an exhausted state fall to her knees and ask the Lord for help and deliverance. She cried aloud and admitted her heart was broken. It was at this point that even as a child I realized she had experienced as much as she could ever stand from her ungrateful and belligerent daughter.

The next day when the prodigal daughter awoke my mother went directly to her room and asked her quietly to leave. Still very much in a half-drunken stupor, the daughter issued forth all kinds of insults ending with, "This is my house too, bitch! I ain't going nowhere!" Calmly, my mother went to her room, reached into her purse and extracted the gun she'd packed the night before to protect her daughter from her plight at the hands of the common-law husband.

Horrified my father asked her, "Where are you going with that?" He struggled to try to follow her and stumped his toe on the edge of the bed. This delayed his arrival at my mother's side long enough for her to take aim at the prodigal daughter from the door of her bedroom. If it had not been for my father's quick intervention, his daughter would have died in her bed that same day. The first shot left the gun before my father began to struggle for possession. It barely missed her and went into the wall above the prodigal daughter's head. While my parents contended for the pistol, she fired several more times. Finally, my father succeeded in taking the gun away. My mother looked at her daughter and coldly stated, "I brought you here, and I will take you out."

Wisely, the prodigal daughter who had been snatched into a sudden state of sobriety, hurriedly packed her many boxes. Usually, it took her days to gather all her prized possessions. This time, she and her vast collection were out the house and in a cab within what must have been less than an hour. She did not return for even a visit for many months to come.

My relationship with my parents never in anyway resembled the one they had with the prodigal daughter. For the remainder of the precious time that I was privileged to be under their care I continued to be exposed to a wide range of emotions and poignant lessons. They never denied I was "nearly-adopted" and they severely admonished any action from me that resembled one they had seen in the prodigal daughter.

The pitfall of drugs and addiction did not find a place in my life because I feared worse than death itself to in anyway be responsible for breaking the heart of my mother. It was drilled into my head by them that I could "do anything you want," and their faith helped me believe that I was someone very special.

My mother and I had many conversations at the foot of the crooked stairway. She'd always take my hand and tell me with tears in her eyes, "All I want you to do is be a good girl."

When the hard days of my life have come down from out of nowhere, it's the scripture she insisted I memorize that I repeat over and over again. She gave me the 23rd Psalm of David and it's her voice I hear in the back of my head leading me away from danger.

My father was very proud of his job as a janitor with IBM. He understood my love of all sorts of gadgets and gizmos and almost every night he'd bring home an interesting looking gear or lever for me to add to my collection. My love for fixing things and tinkering with those pieces of equipment culminated one day as I followed in his footsteps to become a technician with IBM.

They were my parents and I'm proud to say they choose me. As I type these words, my eyes are filled with tears. Now, I'm painfully aware of how much I truly miss them.

CHAPTER 19 -- UNDESERVED KINDNESS

We always found a way to go to the pool, movies and the local YMCA. We accomplished this no matter how many hungry mouths existed in the family or how tight funds were for the household. Word of a planned outing spread rapidly up and down the main street of the Village. It was common for another family to chip-in the expense of an additional admission if one child's parents said they could not afford it. Any trip that involved an extended period of time away from home usually required at least two friends to travel together beyond the edge of the neighborhood. On the other hand, it was not uncommon to make a trip to the grocery store alone at any hour of the day.

We weren't always deserving of the kindness of our parents. In fact we were sometimes hateful and inconsiderate. This fact was evidenced by our unfair treatment of Sadie.

Sadie was a robust, large and terrifying woman who lived at the top of the hill. There were many secrets surrounding Sadie. We were afraid of her and so we tried to cover-up our fear by issuing a flow of never-ending personal slurs in her direction. Her large and protruding backside and big, juicy always-drooling-mouth with yellow and twisted teeth provided topics for the caustic harassment. She suffered abuse from the children and young adults each time she walked down the street. One had to be brave to be Sadie.

The boys of the Village were especially cruel. As they grew older, their verbal abuse became more and more sexual in nature. Sadie was a fighter but limited by a small vocabulary and a severe stutter. She was not in anyway a match for their ever-increasing and piercing insults. It was not in her power to change her appearance or augment her ability to learn. There was a fire in her spirit and we knew that if pushed too far she would retaliate. It was not uncommon for her to even give chase to her persecutors.

The parents of the Village whispered to the children that Sadie was "retarded." This was not a great deal of information for us. After all, we did not have any point of reference to understand that this meant Sadie was a "special" person. In fact, Sadie had the misfortune of being the only child born in the Village for two generations that was in anyway different. Our elders protested our behavior and they showed a lack of tolerance whenever they witnessed one of us trying to persecute Sadie. The parent's warnings were heard but the taunting behavior regarding Sadie continued. It was obvious that our parents were equally puzzled as to exactly how to treat Sadie.

Her mother was a quiet woman who spent most of her days caring for their cozy home. The family was well-mannered and kind. There must have been times that her mother observed the mistreatment of her daughter at the hands of the Village people. One also had to be brave to be Sadie's mother.

Sadie truly loved the babies and the older people of the Village. She always had a kind and polite word for anyone her senior and to whom she knew she should address as "ma'am." The old folks would reply by asking Sadie how she was doing and inquire about the health of her mother. When a new baby arrived, Sadie made a point to pay a visit to the home and take a good look at the new member of the community. It was strange that she always would make a special effort to be kind to the new mother who had probably just recently been one of her tormenters.

The Village was shocked when one day Sadie had her own baby. Rumors spread and names were dropped but the father of Sadie's child was never identified. Her son was not "special" like his mother. Instead, he grew to exhibit a quiet, gentle and thoughtful nature similar to that of his grandmother. Sadie continued to be bombarded by slurs which only increased after the birth of her baby. Each generation of Village children devised a signature and disgusting way of dealing with Sadie.

In the end, the Village was forced to admit that Sadie had held a position that only resembled acceptance within our ranks. Actually, it would be more accurate to say she never even came close. The day she died we all filed by her casket. We, the "normal" Village members universally had to admit, "We should've been nicer to Sadie."

Our parents seemed to always be fighting to do the right thing. They tried to persuade us to be generous by showing generosity towards us. We had struggled to resist the temptation to make fun of Sadie. After her death, we were now more aware of the fact that we should never mistreat another person just because they are not like us. Our gross misbehavior did not stop them from depositing whatever money they could into our waiting hands.

The end of the school year was marked by an annual picnic at West View Amusement Park. The rides cost as much as a dime. For this amount it was even possible to have the living day-lights literally scared out of you if you were brave enough to take a whirl on the infamous roller coaster called the Racing Whippet. The parents rarely even ventured into the area of the park that contained the rides. They were content to sit in the picnic area and talk over the heaping picnic baskets.

During the summer, we spent the funds on popsicles and other treats. It was agreed that our favorite pastime was swimming. The walk to the pool extended almost four miles. It involved many shortcuts through the cool, wooded acreage that grew in abundance close to the edge of a winding back road. Eventually, the street gently passed the base of the park where the swimming pool was located. All that was needed was a bath towel, swimming suit and a little extra money for a bag of chips to tide you over on the long walk back home. The pool was huge with a deep end that exceeded a depth of twelve feet. It was used as an informal staging area for many diving and racing events. In addition, it was the most desirable spot to cool off during the humid and hot summer.

A fee had to be paid as admission to the chain link fence gated pool in exchange for a large safety pin with a number embossed on it. The number indicated which basket on a shelf in the dressing room should be used to store dry street clothes. The floor in the dressing room and the required shower were always very cold. A good day at the pool lasted for hours. Naturally, we found it hard to walk after being in water for such a long time. We laughed at each other as we wobbled and struggled to regain our ground legs. The skin on our fingers and feet was wrinkled by the water. It was only then that we felt it was time to go home.

We did not understand how hard our parents had to work to earn the money we so freely spent. In addition to this, most of us felt somehow entitled to behave badly while accepting their undeserved generosity. I don't remember actually tormenting Sadie, but I did harbor an unnatural fear to be around her. She probably sensed this each time I avoided acknowledging her greetings by rudely turning my entire head in another direction. I'm ashamed to admit that sometimes I snatched my head so quickly and violently away from her that I'm surprised I didn't break my neck.

My personal legacy, because of my gross mistreatment of Sadie, has been to fight a lifetime battle to be kind. I continue to struggle in order to avoid even starting to pass judgment when dealing with everyone. Perhaps now, I won't fail another human being as miserably as I did fail Sadie.

CHAPTER 20 -- A KEEPING BUSY ETHIC

Summer was thoroughly planned by the adults of the Village to incorporate positive learning experiences. Above all, they tried to keep us busy. Their purpose was to help us avoid falling victim to some self-initiated catastrophe. The Village adults firmly believed that "Idle hands are a devil's workshop." Rarely were we permitted to simply while away the lazy summer afternoon in front of a buzzing television.

Mornings started a bit later than during a normal school day. There was always a special vacation chore assignment to be completed before any thought was given to the remainder of the day. We were expected to dress and get ready to go to the library, YMCA or day-camp. If our grades were not high enough the previous year, it was absolutely certain that we would be obligated to attend summer school. It was ill-advised for you to be caught standing still too long or looking as if the day was boring. All adults in the Village were part of a united front. It was not uncommon for them to brag that they could always find something for an ungrateful child to do.

Laziness, a lack of gratitude and back-talking always demanded harsh punishment. Often, the best approach to being a child in the Village was to pretend you were invisible. Generally, we preferred to avoid the adults. It was too easy to cross over a line and enter the zone of misbehaving. They all shared a very low level of tolerance. Most of them could issue a multi-blow "switching" while simultaneously daring you to even look like you wanted to cry. Others were known to grab the first object they could put their hands on to level punishment. All this was legal and expected. It was not viewed as damaging by the church or society. The rod was not spared in order to prevent us from being spoiled.

Every child in the Village had to take swimming lessons at the local YMCA. The more fortunate of us were able to participate in a six week session of summer camp at this facility. It was also here that we were first exposed to trampolines, pool tables, basketball, weight-lifting and many other healthy diversions that would become for some of us lifetime obsessions. The environment was loosely supervised. We did not have a tendency to argue or fight. Damage to the property only happened by accident and vandalism wasn't a consideration. The Y was integrated. It never occurred to anyone in the community to change anything about the way things were being run at the organization.

In sports the children were equal. It was rare to see one team composed of only Village children when the teams were chosen. Athletic talent, the ability to deliver a consistent performance, and the desire to win were recognized, encouraged and admired within the building. Outside the Y's glass and brick structure, elements of the Village and neighborhood continued for the most part to be happily unaware of one another's hopes and aspirations.

One of my peers spent countless hours in the gym lifting weights with his legs. We watched him in amazement while he repeatedly asked that more resistance be added. He was thin and unimposing when he first came to the Y. Slowly and meticulously his physical prowess and mental attitude were transformed. Soon after high school, he had a very successful college career in Texas as an All American and went on to play for a professional football team. During his slow physical development he was never heard to utter one word regarding a desire to make millions of dollars. At that time in the history of American athletic competition, the professionals still played the game simply because they loved it.

The parental objective to keep us busy and to avoid idle hands worked well for most of us. Unfortunately, a few of my peers were not impressed by their efforts or the punishment that was applied to their rear ends. It would not take long for the parents to see exactly what their hard earned investment of cash and caring could produce.

CHAPTER 21 – The 60's INFLEXIBILITY

Every child in the Village was repeatedly encouraged to dream. At the same time, we were told to latch on to the tools required to reach our desired destination. We received an equal education in an award winning school district, and we participated in Brownies, Girl Scouts and Boy Scouts at the sides of our neighborhood peers. The diversity of our environment was evidenced by the many dialects and ethnic flavors that surrounded us. The melodic mixture of languages alone supported the idea that a life beyond the divisive bush was possible. One element remained unmentionable. Without confronting or even being exposed to it we were hindered from making any meaningful progress. Our church, our parents and the school system totally neglected to provide any Negro specific historical information.

The city fathers of "The Steel City" seemed to believe that they had suffered long under the watchful eyes of a vigilant black owned newspaper, the *Pittsburgh Courier*. The strongly opinionated periodical began to be published in 1902. Its mission was to represent the Negro community in every aspect of our lives. Repeatedly, the white owned and operated newspapers detailed efforts by the politicians to provide an apparent environment of equality. The Courier told the truth about how little was actually being gained by these efforts.

The courtrooms were the battlefields. In them decisions were made that seemed to promote and nurture only an uneasy racial harmony between the ethnically diverse populations of the vast and sprawling city. These were the reasons that for the most part a visit from Martin Luther King, Jr. was viewed by many in the neighborhood and Village as being totally unnecessary and potentially disruptive during the early 1960's.

"What do you think he thinks he's gonna do around here?" It was my mother who posed this question with a bit of sarcasm in her voice while bracing herself for an unknown response from anyone who would listen. "You know what I really hate about that man? He's always flying into some town and getting everybody all stirred up then the next thing you know, he's somewhere else and leaving the cleanin' up to the people that live there." She never said whether or not she believed in the non-violent approach he encouraged in his many passionate speeches. It was obvious that in her viewpoint his behavior could only be described as cowardly.

She expressed horror regarding the reported lynchings and general maltreatment of colored people that was being reported by the press from her native

South. Above all, she sincerely believed that in the North, where she now lived, things were not in any way as primitive. Dr. King's ability to rock the boat on which she sat was definitely a change to which she did not wish to aspire.

The information she had regarding Dr. King was obtained from reading the *Pittsburgh Courier*, *Life Magazine*, *Ebony Magazine*, *Jet Magazine*, the *Pittsburgh Post Gazette* and television. It was my mother's opinion that the most reliable source for news was the new kid in town, television. During this volatile era, TV journalistic snippets and bits of information started to influence the American psyche. We were in the first stages of becoming dependent upon the black and white picture tube that dominated most of our living-rooms.

After all, the creditability of live-video could not be denied. Somehow, the desire for a complete explanation began to slip away. This questionable influence did modify the behavior of my mother. Prior to the arrival of the TV, my mother had been a woman who believed first in the word of God. Now, she was likely to quote something she'd heard Walter Cronkite say last night on the news into a chastisement as she would one of her beloved scriptures.

CHAPTER 22 -- REBELLION

The beautiful homes of various styles in the neighborhood reflected the fact that is was an ethnic mixture of first and second generation Italians, Poles, and Germans.   Despite the overall beauty that surrounded them, they always seemed to be involved in some form of "white-on-white" or "white-on-black" persecution. It was common for the Germans to taunt the Poles for being stupid and for both these groups to turn on the Italians and accuse them of being smelly. We, the Village inhabitants were a prime and easy target. It wasn't uncommon to hear the "N" word, nigger. The despicable term was launched indiscriminately and often without provocation.

Our parents were sometimes taunted by the children of their white employers. The most painful harassments were not overt. The fact that our mothers mended their clothes, cleaned their toilets and cooked their food didn't stop some of our schoolmates. They were especially fond of making fun of the thick southern accents of our mothers. Fortunately, most members of the neighborhood did not participate or approve of this type of behavior. They were the majority. Therefore, their disapproval made it unpopular to openly mistreat any resident of the Village. However, the mean-spirited tormenters found creative ways to roll their eyes and insult us.

It was now the Summer of 1960 and the tables were beginning to be turned on our loose and fowl-mouthed classmates. Verbal confrontations increased. We no longer sat quietly on the sidelines. We refused to be quite and accepting. The attempts to help us define our position in society based on rules given to us by the majority were under suspicion. A few friendships in school between Black and white classmates had started to develop. However, our new friends still did not come to visit our homes. This was despite the fact that a few of us were now welcomed into their houses by their mothers.

At some point, I began to believe that I was more than a citizen of only the Village. Our parents never spoke of their lot in life except to repeat how grateful they were to not live back in the South. The oppressive hedge now had a parallel chain-link fence and drainage gully. Yet, it never became a hot topic of discussion. Whenever given the opportunity, our parents made sure we were on the right path. They reminded us constantly of the importance of a good education. They assured us that once we earned as much of this precious commodity as possible, we would never have to worry about feeling as good as anyone else on the face of the earth.

Village children were expected to attend college. We were instructed that a college education was the key to success and freedom. Dropping out of school did happen in the Village. When it did, the perpetrator had to contend with only one question repeated to him or her over and over again, "Why?" It is possible that the parents and guardian-parents valued the children for many reasons. We knew without being told that we were their salvation.

Everything that year bored me. My mother's wisdom seemed stupid and old fashioned. I absolutely had everything figured out. I didn't dare confront my mother and tell her I thought she was dated. I wisely restricted myself to rolling my eyes behind her back. Most of the time, I simply refused to listen to anything she had to say. She realized that I had changed and warned me that God requires children to, "respect their elders." I didn't "talk back," but I did think enough bad thoughts to deserve her tongue lashings. I am now convinced that my wise parents probably realized I wasn't listening. I'm also positive that they realized that I wasn't half as smart as I thought I was at that time my life.

I was still fascinated by the neighborhood. Girl Scouts and I had by then gone our separate ways. Resigning from the troop was one of the ways I established myself as being too old for foolish things. Along with this relationship went the yearly cookie drives. One of the few remaining ways that I could now actually get a peak inside the homes was during our candy runs to the neighborhood during Halloween. The only other time I approached the front doors of those grand houses was when I delivered a message or parcel for my mother.

Homes in the neighborhood were multi-storied. The majority sat back a substantial distance from the sidewalk. The approach to the houses typically consisted of a walkway and a stairwell from that walkway that extended to a broad porch. Green or gray colored blinds surrounded many of the porches. These lucky families appeared to have everything. They could spend refreshing late afternoons and early evenings during the summer watching the world go by from a cooled refuge. A few of the homes even had porch swings sitting in a cozy corner. When you passed by the houses you could hear the swings creaking and even listen to the muffled conversations.

The unfortunate truth at this time was that still there was no real personal intercommunication between the neighborhood and the Village. This was despite the fact that Village residents had made some progress towards equality in the community. The butcher would inquire about the health of your mother and father. The pharmacist knew exactly who you were and what medicines your family required. Grocery clerks reminded you that your mother preferred a certain type of coffee. We understood that they held a great deal of knowledge about who we were and what they thought we wanted. This intimate knowledge operated to their advantage. It was not a two way street. We knew very little about them. It was impossible to do anything without walking through the neighborhood. We had to pass their homes if we wanted to go shopping, go to school, or catch a bus for any reason. Observing us was done consistently and without apologies.

As we matured, we became acutely aware of the diligent observation tactics of the adults in the neighborhood. This revelation on our part drastically altered our prospective regarding the neighborhood as a place of escape. A walk to the store had become a walk under pressure. We were beginning to strongly dislike their intrusive profiling. At some point, we realized we were being observed for reasons other than our well-being.

Each parent in the Village that worked held some sort of job that required a form of personal sacrifice and often humiliation. Several of our fathers were employed in one of the huge steel mills that surrounded Pittsburgh. Generally, they were given jobs that required them to work dangerously close to the raging ovens.

Most of our mothers cooked and cleaned in homes within the neighborhood. This required them to travel by streetcar or bus for hours to reach the really elite mansions in one of the very rich sections of the city. Only two of the female members of the Village were professionals. One was a nurse at the local small hospital in our community. The other worked for the post office as a supervisor. They occupied a special place in the hearts of the community. Both women were industrious spirits. For many reasons, we children were inspired by watching their comings and goings. Each week they traveled in their own cars into the inner city. While there, they regularly had their hair and nails done. We loved to go into their homes just to smell the exotic perfumes they wore. Both served every Sunday as deaconesses at church.

We talked in small groups during the long summer evenings under streetlights. Most of the time, we discussed what we hoped to do and where we planned to go when we finally left the Village. There never seemed to be any doubt that most of us had no intention or desire to remain in the Village a moment longer than it would take us to get a job or go off to college. The older we got the more obvious it became to us that we lived in a place that was surrounded by a neighborhood that never had much interest in accepting us under any circumstances.

A cause for concern and resentment to the Village was the fact that the transit authority conveniently provided only the neighborhood direct access to the suburbs and downtown. The system consisted of an electrically driven, noisy trolley car that jerked and weaved its way along a set of recessed tracks. My family was like most of the families in the Village because we relied exclusively on public transportation. It was necessary to walk to the center of the neighborhood and stand in front of one of their houses to wait for the trolley. You could feel their prying eyes evaluating the modest outfit you wore. You could sense their objection to our presence in their domain.

The subtle and overt insults only increased over the years. They didn't have to put a foot inside our homes in order to determine what type of people they thought we were. Our characters could be judged simply by putting two and two together after observing us day after day. Conversely, our white neighbors remained for us an enigma. They held the power of information over us like a hammer. Eventually, it was only natural that someone from the Village would attempt a bold act of rebellion against the neighborhood. I felt that the revolt would only be valid and important if it was accomplished while the observers peered intently through the windows of their comfortable houses.

As do many acts of rebellion, this one started innocently enough. It was due in part to the well-meaning generosity of my unsuspecting mother. Most of our parents had not been able to remain in school beyond the 5th or 6th grade. It was amazing that they seemed to feel it was not really important what they had to do in order to make a way for the children. These same parents would reach deeply into their nearly empty pockets and generously dispense to the children money to go to the movies, amusement parks or to ride the trolleys downtown almost without hesitation.

The revolution began on an unusually cool and breezy August evening. I was surprised and delighted when my mother decided to give me a tremendous present. She proudly handed me enough cash to purchase cokes and pizza for a group of friends. I spread the word quickly. Shortly after sundown, we met near the divisive hedge at the edge of the Village. We were a noisy and happy group of more than a dozen as we made our way to the tiny deli and combo ice cream parlor in the heart of the neighborhood.

The boys amused themselves along the way to the pizza shop by pushing and teasing the girls. The girls shoved the boys back and threatened to beat them within an inch of their lives if they touched them again. Both groups joked and laughed mostly about what we were going to do the first day back to school. Fall session was scheduled to start in less than a month.

For some reason that evening, I was distracted and especially sensitive to the unseen eyes of the neighborhood. My parents and I had never stolen or even thought about stealing anything from their stores. I had always behaved in a respectful manner towards white adults even when I was called a nigger. They had nothing to fear from me. In fact, my mother constantly warned me to watch my behavior closely whenever I was around white people. She tried to explain her opinion by adding that they just didn't even want to understand anything about us.

What crimes had I or my friends committed that merited such attention? During Halloween, the streams of toilet paper that draped their yards as tricks were placed there by their own children. I couldn't recall one case of any crime against them being committed by anyone in the Village. Unsuccessfully, I tried to push aside the strange feelings of ill-will. My friends probably didn't have any idea that these thoughts were running through my head. My demeanor remained upbeat on the way to the pizza parlor.

We placed our orders and then each of us selected a bottled soda. The comforting smell of oregano and fresh pepperoni filled the small building. Some of us remained inside to watch the cook prepare the pizza. This particular employee had developed a reputation for effortlessly tossing pizza dough. His performances were fluid. Usually, his gentle and high throws of the soft and pliable dough were done in time with the music of a small portable radio. The popular stations during this time were all found on the AM band. Music simply lacked almost any bass quality. We also thought it was normal for the signal to fade at anytime. The dough and treble dominated music failed to attract my interest. I couldn't stop thinking about all the meddling eyes of the neighborhood.

I exited the shop and stood underneath the awning as the pizza entered the oven. I could hear the voice of my mother in my mind warning me to never step over the line with "those people." But I decided I didn't care. I just wanted to strike back. I started to concoct a plan that I felt would really give those many eyes something to see. Most of my group of friends by this time had also decided to come outside to wait on their slice of pizza. Confidence filled me as I turned to them and announced, "Hey guys, I know what we should do. What do you think will happen if we put our coke bottles on the streetcar tracks?" At first, I thought they were ignoring me. I repeated my idea and a few of them only began to laugh and tease me about what they quickly labeled a stupid idea.

The pizza was soon ready and I went back inside to pay. We ate and began to walk slowly back to the Village. I guess my friends also heard the voices of their parents in their heads. They munched the hot, cheesy slices at first without responding to my suggestion. I was not discouraged. I simply kept repeating my proposal to the group. Soon, a few of them were convinced. Only two started to walk faster in order to avoid being involved. I was beyond caring about their lack of interest and protests. One of them gave it one last try by saying, "What do you think will happen? They'll break when the streetcar runs over them. Then we'll be in big trouble."

The largest intersection was just a block away from the pizza parlor. It was well lit and there were neighborhood houses on all four corners. To make my point, I stopped in the middle of the street and boldly put my soda bottle right in the middle of the streetcar tracks. Truthfully, I didn't care what would happen if the trolley hit the bottles. I was on one of those missions in which the means are justified by the end. The result I wanted was for the neighborhood to know that I was responsible for this act. After this day, they would have to admit that someone from the Village was not going to take it anymore.

My teen years were just beginning. I had always been quiet and non-imposing in front of my parents and other adults. I believed that I was successful at keeping my real feelings inside. I didn't think that my parents realized or cared that I was now full of a false sense of confidence. Above all, I really believed that I had mysteriously acquired all the answers. I wasn't interested in even listening to personal criticism or advice from anyone. The years of wise warnings from my parents had been devalued and carelessly thrown somewhere to the back of my mind. It was for these reasons that I now felt I had a right to be more than mildly angered by the attitude of the pious and truly uncaring white members of my community.

On one hand, I also realized that there would be hell to pay. There was absolutely no way I would be able to deny my actions. After all, my plan included the required observation of our protest by the neighborhood residents. We would be identified. I kept insisting and my friends soon became willing followers. They laughed and began to put their bottles between the tracks. I had learned a valuable lesson about leadership. A strong leader has to just provide the initial idea and the masses will soon follow. I remember feeling very proud of myself as we casually strolled back to the Village.

The result of our actions soon came home to roost and exact a toll. The neighborhood rallied and notified the police. The officers brought a paddy wagon to the Village and we were herded into it right in front of our shocked parents. The sirens and lights were turned on as the van moved slowly through the neighborhood to the local precinct. Once at the police station, we were deposited inside a huge holding cell. Some of us began to cry and regret our actions. The police didn't even have to verbally threaten my now guilt-ridden cohorts. They simply stood stern-faced in front of us with their arms crossed. The regrets of my friends soon turned into confessions. The officers simply listened to the facts and quickly identified me as the source of the problem. At this point, they immediately placed me in a cell alone.

The police did not immediately question me. It seemed like hours passed before they appeared outside my cell. I made my mind up to look them directly in the eye and above all I would not cry. I knew the facts and I was sure I could live with whatever was about to happen. There would be punishment at the hands of my mother. I was sure this would be delivered to my behind by one of the switches that I would have to pick myself from a tree in our yard. I planned to bravely bare the pain. I still believed that what I had done was right. I had used the time alone in the cell to become even stronger in my convictions.

The policemen's uniforms did intimidate me. I never thought they would actually harm me but I kept an eye on their holstered firearms. One of the two officers began to slowly and quietly speak. "So, young lady, this was all your big idea?" He looked down at me and calmly repeated, "You don't have to tell us. We know it was you that started this whole thing."
As planned, I did not resort to crying. Instead, I respectfully looked him directly in his eyes without saying a word.

"Well, we thought you'd like to know that all your friends have gone home. That's right, their parents have come to get them and they are probably already back in their houses by now." He paused for a minute to see if I was going to respond. When I didn't say anything he continued, "That leaves us with you to deal with."

He told me that the Village parents had been apologetic and genuinely embarrassed by the action of their children. I was frightened but still very proud of myself. He finally began to explain what I was really facing. "Well, it appears we've got a problem as far as you're concerned. Nobody seems to want to accept custody of you." It was at this point that I became afraid. What did he mean there was nobody? My demeanor must have suddenly changed because he quickly added, "Oh, now you're paying attention. That's right. Your parents told us to keep you. In fact, your mother did come here to the police station. But after telling us to lock you up and throw away the key, she simply left. What do you think about that?"

I never thought that this would be a possibility. How could she?

"The good news for you is that we can't keep you. What you did was horrible but it is not worthy of your being sent to Juvenile Court. So, this leaves us with the responsibility to try to convince your mother to take you back. Do you understand?"

I most definitely understood. Now, I began to cry. The ring-leader and idea person hadn't won respect after all. Instead, I was in serious jeopardy of losing everything.

My mother did not have an ounce of fear in her heart for any man. She was the one who had always insisted that I always look everyone directly in the eye. I was not confused by her behavior because I knew she didn't view white people as animals. For example, her advice regarding angry dogs was just the opposite; I was told to never stare directly into the eyes of any wild animal. Her belief that you should pay close attention when another human being is talking remained strong. This was despite the fact that so many white people during that period felt that black people were little more than advanced apes. Therefore, white people were always viewed by me as human and worth my complete attention.

The police officers abruptly left and did not return for hours. I woke from a light sleep and realized it was now early morning. I could see sunbeams reflected against the drab grey ceiling above my cot. I heard my mother's voice and that of the officers approaching my cell. When they again stood in front of me the officer repeated, "It still looks like she doesn't want you." At this point they faced my mother and asked her, "You want to tell her, to her face what you told us we should do with her?"

My mother promptly replied, "Like I told you last night and on the phone again, that's up to you." This firm retort remained her only reply. The policemen continued to try to get her to agree to take me home. She finally relented. I could see that she genuinely did not want me to go with her. For the first time, I heard her say something that revealed to me exactly what she thought about her position in society. Glaring and full of anger and disappointment, she boldly stared into the eyes of one of the officers and said, "I told that girl over and over the same thing about trouble. I thought she understood that it ain't bad to have something to say about things that really bother you. You have to pick your fights and this here thing hasn't done nothing but put her in a bad position. She don't have no business here in your jail and she knows it."

They were obviously grateful to release me into her custody. The paperwork took another half hour and during this time they had very little to say to her. I sat in a hard wooden chair by her side. I felt her resentment for both me and these men permeate the entire room. She made absolutely no attempt to hide her emotions. We had talked many times about the way I thought the white people watched everything we did. Most of the time when we had these often one sided conversations she didn't comment. The most she ever said was, "Well, we have to be grateful for what we've got." I desperately wanted to believe that she knew that in my mind I felt my behavior was justified.

On the long walk back to the Village she continued to reprimand me. "I told you I don't want to have any dealings with them damn people. I never, ever want to go to them with my hat in my hand. Look what you've done to yourself. Now they know who you are, Miss Lady. And you'll see this ain't no good thing."

The punishment was extensive and prolonged. I never developed a feeling of shame for the act of rebellion itself but I did come to regret that in the end it seemed to have proven absolutely nothing. The real lesson gained regarding this incident was based on my mother's viewpoint. I was now aware that it is always ill advised to place yourself totally at the will of the very people to which you wish to demonstrate opposition.

Over the next few months, she often expressed outrage and a deep sense of disappointment. I never was given a hint of encouragement for my behavior. Instead, she would occasionally remind me that I was expected to always strive to be outstanding and different. The majority of the time, she continued to bitterly remind me of my foolishness if I failed to perform the tiniest of her demands. Periodically, when she was relaxed she would patiently explain that the mandate to be unique did not exclude being righteously rebellious. It did exclude being stupid.

My supposed revolt did reveal that I was not ready to rely strictly on my own ability to make good decisions. The revolution against the neighborhood had gone too far. I was told in no uncertain terms that my rash act had put at risk the critical Village goal for all the children. A new sadness in my mother's eyes reminded me that she was justifiably concerned about my future. The revolution had the potential to destroy our clean and proud exit from the oppressive community.

There were many long walks ahead of me through the now hostile neighborhood. Our white neighbors continued to be vigilant and overly concerned. Some of them had tried to act nonchalant in the past. Now, many of them seemed to go out of their way to show us they were paying close attention to our behavior.

I now completely understood my mother's hopes. I too began to look more towards the future. I knew that one day my frequent and familiar steps through enemy territory would eventually take me beyond this unbalanced society and into a true community. I became an optimist about this outside and unfamiliar place. Naively, I saw it as a sanctuary. I was convinced that it would be there that I would finally find an open wooden and glass door on each elevated and welcoming porch.

CHAPTER 23 -- SAM AND STEVE

Each child in the Village approached the challenge of growing up differently. Most of us tried to establish ourselves in some way as being unique. Our parents rented musical instruments, paid team fees and encouraged us to participate in every field trip offered during the school year. We were able to attend symphonies, co-op classes in physics and biology, and even participated in theatrical festivals at the University of Pittsburgh. We certainly appeared to be a generation that was destined to go somewhere.

There wasn't any way for our parents to predict which ones of us would achieve successful and happy lives. In the end, it didn't seem to matter whether or not we chose to focus on sports or intellectual pursuits. Even from the beginning, the challenge to find our way would prove too much for some of us.

Two examples come to mind that more then illustrate this point. One of them would prove to be intellectually gifted while the other preferred to exhibit his physical prowess on the football field. They both had many talents in a variety of areas. However, it is fair to say that they operated at different ends of the behavioral spectrum. In fact, during their early years, both Sam and Steve behaved in a way best described by the fictional character Forest Gump. "Stupid is as stupid does."

Steve's parents were upper-middle class members of the Village society. The clothes he wore and the bicycles he rode were all first-rate. It was believed that Steve had many friends in the neighborhood. To those of us that faced him everyday he was a boisterous, insulting and pushy bully. At one time, every child in the Village had fallen victim to one or another of Steve's many warped pranks and peculiar plans. It was not wise to trust Steve. Eventually, he would make it impossible.

The house Steve lived in was the first brand new home to be built in the Village during my generation. It was a traditional split foyer with a full basement and garage. Steve was determined to use the basement to his advantage. Whenever his parents left home, he would quickly spread the word around the Village that he was having a party. Unlike most of the boys of the Village, Steve was not content to simply pull the ponytails of the girls. His gross and distasteful attempts to attract the opposite sex were beyond description. Steve's groping hands and threats to lick our bodies with his long, slimy tongue were for most of us our first sexually offensive and frustrating experience.

Any description of Steve should include the fact that he was a large and muscular young man with shifty eyes. Trying to look directly into Steve's eyes was an impossible task that none of us aspired to achieve. We knew Steve was dangerous despite his sharp clothes and what appeared to be his many athletic and social connections. Whenever there was a fight or disagreement, Steve was not always directly involved but he was always present. The Village boys were constantly in search of a safe place to be alone with their constantly rotating girlfriend of the week. Steve often had access to his parent's home because they had to work double and sometimes triple shifts. It was primarily for this reason that the boys allowed him to believe that he was their leader.

In many ways, Steve's idea of leadership strongly resembled that of the Mafia. He maintained a caste system – you were either "in or out." Once in, forget about getting back out. Just like a Don of a Mafioso brotherhood, Steve made all the contacts for the group and established his sense of style and etiquette. The followers of Steve occupied an elite level of his imposed caste system. They could be identified by their scorn and harsh treatment of any outsider. You were an outsider if you did not serve a purpose for the entire group or for any one of them individually.

It was very easy for Steve to travel throughout the city because he always seemed to have money. Therefore, he established "partyin' contacts" all over the metropolitan Pittsburgh area. Some of the Village adults just knew that one day Steve would go somewhere exciting, or do something extremely important. His prowess on the football field and his charismatic personality simply left most of the adults speechless. We, his peers, had other expectations for Steve. In the presence of one of the "Steve fans" we simply sat, waited, and listened.

One thing was obvious, Steve's parents appeared to really love both him and his younger sister. His mother was one of the few professionals in the Village and his father worked at the post office. They were known to take vacations to visit relatives throughout the entire country. It appeared to all members of the Village that Steve's father and mother invested lots of money and time in their children. The house was always elaborately decorated for the holidays. Steve and his parents maintained a meticulous manicured yard. Their grass was religiously cut each summer weekend. It was observed with pride by many of the Village adults that Steve's house could have easily been transplanted to the neighborhood. Unfortunately, the family would not have been allowed to migrate with it.

A fence surrounded Steve's house in the back. Behind that fence they kept an unusual dog. The beast pulled sentry duty with a vengeance. Most families in the Village either owned a pet or they shared the obligation to provide meals for the pets of their neighbors. Everyone did this because it was expected. We understood it to be our responsibility to care for animals because they could not care for themselves. Therefore, it was a common sight to see a dog following its owner to and from the bus stop. Scrubby, almost wild cats also freely enjoyed meals at every backdoor in the Village. The feral cats and neighbors alike avoided even approaching Steve's backdoor.

On the other hand, Steve's family held the distinction of providing a home for an animal that was so mean that it was rumored that the dog might even be possessed by a daemon. The rear of their house was in the middle of the block in the alley that divided the Village. Everyone used the alley as a shortcut. As we passed Steve's house, the rabid dog would snarl, growl and often throw himself into the fence in a fit of rage. Crime was not a problem in the Village. So, it was only natural that our parents often wondered why such a sweet family needed and seemed to love that vulgar and vicious excuse for a dog.

Perhaps, one of the girls in the Village may have loved Steve. Not one of us would ever admit to this if it were true. Universally, we all complained to each other about his distasteful behavior. Everything he did usually turned into an excuse for him to try to drag one of us back to the den he had made of his parent's basement.

Many things changed as we grew older. However, we never tired of playing games under the street lights in the early evening. During the course of the day, we usually agreed to meet beneath one of the lampposts and vote which game to play. Hide-and-go-seek was the overall favorite. Steve was at least two years older than most of us. This didn't stop him for creeping out of the shadows to insist that we honor him by playing by his rules. The harmless game would then become something warped.

During those long summer evenings, we girls had more to be afraid of than simply being tagged. Always horny Steve was known as the local prowler. He made the game something ugly and dirty. We knew his real objective was to find some way to satisfy himself. The girls who wanted to continue to play resigned themselves to avoid hiding in any dark corner. I could not abide being around Steve. So, I usually quit without even offering an explanation to anyone. He was already one of those pitiful men that women recognize as a grinder. Steve was happy if he just got to put his clothed penis on any girl and rub it on her anywhere.

As the years went by Steve's gang began to wander. The boys of the Village had made their own connections. At some point, he became a very serious problem to his parents. Finally, he succeeded in becoming a concern for the entire community. His slide into fame was officially documented. The grief that he brought to his parents would be described as beyond expectation.

Somewhere along the way, Steve decided to join a movement that did not exist in the Village. The outside connections that he'd spent countless hours cultivating were to provide for him the means to finally bring him to his knees. The signs were there and now it can be said that Steve was at the very least an addictive personality.

It didn't take him long to begin a relationship with cocaine. While his peers went off to college or to fight a war in Vietnam, Steve roved the streets of Pittsburgh and got higher and higher. Soon, he found himself in jail. Arrest followed arrest. The charges ranged from simple possession to possession for resale. One day he achieved the classification of three-time loser. The judge without any reservations simply threw the key away. It is for this reason and much more that he has always held and still holds the unfortunate position of being our greatest under-achiever.

Sam was the exact opposite. He was a genius. The term "geek" was not known at that time. If it had existed, we would have surely used this to taunt him. He wore rather thick glasses from a young age. This fact probably helped him a great deal since he excelled in every academic subject. Sam was a ponytail puller and a butt pincher. He relentlessly teased and harassed every girl in the Village. His size wasn't imposing and he had a head full of what they used to call "good hair." Over the years, Sam had many fights with the boys and the girls of his Village. The frequent confrontations occurred because he had a rare talent for simply getting on everyone's nerves.

Perhaps Sam's behavior can be explained if it is taken into consideration that he was the middle child of a huge family. Middle children seem to crave attention. This is probably due to the fact that under most circumstances within their family they are invisible. Outside his home, Sam was determined to be noticed. The Village adults knew he was truly unique and special. When they were frustrated with one of us about a bad grade, they would ask us, "Why can't you be more like Sam?" What they didn't understand was that we didn't want to be anything like Sam.

The truth is Sam never fit into Steve's world because he was not a follower. Childhood is the time in life when all you really want is to be accepted. Sam single-handedly and successfully did everything he could to avoid peer admiration. Acceptance for him was out of the question. Whether or not this was a purposeful act is not important. I now realize that Sam was probably the first really unique individual that I ever met.

Music seemed to inspire Sam even though he danced with the grace of a block of wood. I once asked him to teach me a simple dance known as the pony. He went into his house and got the record player and a long extension cord. After plugging everything up and plopping the 45 rpm record onto the spindle, he told me to look and learn. I watched him thrash the air, jerk and twist as he did some dance that in no way resembled the pony that I'd seen performed on *Dick Clark's American Bandstand*. His eyes were closed and most of the time he failed to make one move on the beat. He didn't even notice when I left the porch.

Sam was not beneath whining or exaggeration. Yet, he was the smart one and this was not appreciated by me or any of my peers. We girls didn't have to try to avoid Sam. We all knew his fighting skills were a step lower than his dancing ability. When he dared to push us or pull our hair, he would be lucky to escape our wrath. Many times, we even chased him all the way to his door, into his home and waited for him at the foot of his stairs while daring him to set foot in the street ever again. But this did not stop Sam.

When we were growing up not one of us would admit to liking let alone loving Sam. It was a time when all you wanted to be was cool. Sam was definitely not cool. At some point, this all changed when he became the first one of us to enter the University of Pittsburgh. His ability to complete the rigorous engineering curriculum was never in question. It was expected. After all, his outstanding academic performance throughout high school was now a legend.

The rest of us were by then young adults. We were soon to discover that an opinion about anyone is never written in stone. It is something that is subject to change without notice.

During his freshman year, the news circulated through the Village that Sam was having serious problems trying to maintain his grade point average. We still remembered being the victims of his many pranks. However, we now realized that we had to support him. The childhood bitterness towards him gradually began to fade. Our tones changed when we proudly told tales of spitballs he'd thrown or bubblegum he'd placed beneath our seats on the bus. Sam's constant unprovoked harassments had become the stuff used to compose legends. I confess to feeling weird whenever I said something positive about him. The internal conflict and uncomfortable feeling of doing something noble seemed to ease with each new compliment or anecdote I began to freely share about him.

This was one time, like so many more times to come, that we, the almost-adult-Village-children would have to admit that the Village adults probably were right at least some of the time about some things. Everyone probably couldn't get beyond the old image they had in their minds of Sam as nothing less than a jerk. However, the prayers of most of the adults and children of the Village did seem to combine to work in his behalf. Sam rallied and graduated with honors.

CHAPTER 24 -- TYRANTS AND THEIR TERRITORY

Each season held its own magic for the children of the Village. We all possessed active imaginations and used them to devise unique games. Whatever the game there was always an associated hierarchy established amongst the players based on their ability to remember the "rules." Matters were made even more confusing because of the gathering by us of area specific rules for each and every game. Skill was a great part of the equation. All too often, a win could depend on the pecking order of the participants.

A simple game of marbles was not started until there was an agreement reached as to which set of rules should govern the play. The objective of the game is to knock as many of your opponent's marbles out of a circle drawn around them in the dirt. Each player had a special marble larger than the marbles he'd put in the circle that was called a "shooter." Players started by placing their smaller marbles together inside the circle.

They then took turns using their "shooter" to try to knock only their opponent's marbles outside the circle. When you were able to knock an opponent's marble out it became yours. The final winner was the one who at the end of the game had the most marbles.

The game sounds simple enough until you apply "Philadelphia" or "Boston" rules. Any aspect of the game could fall victim to definition. The thickness of the border drawn in the dirt; how many of what color and type of marble you could insert in the middle; how long you could tense your thumb to take a shot with your "shooter," are just a few examples. All these and more variable regulations were debated vigorously with each turn taken. Fist fights and crying jags weren't uncommon.

The girls jumped rope, played jacks and tried to avoid the sun and moist heat in the early afternoon. The street through the middle of the Village gradually elevated from an entrance base at the bottom near the divisive hedge. At the top of the street and just around the corner was a shaded area used by the boys to play baseball. Summer mornings were spent riding your bike through the Village and all over the neighborhood. The northwest side of Pittsburgh is typical of the rest of the city. There is an abundance of steep hills. We were masters of standing, leaning and sliding into the curves to gain the maximum of speed on our roller skates. Every day had the potential to provide another scar and the opportunity to wear a brand new Band-Aid.

As pre-teen Village girls we basically enjoyed spending long afternoons gossiping and planning the next shopping expedition. We did this until the time came to select teams to play kickball or some other sport. We were haunted by the memory of being restricted to standing at the side of the road together watching when we were too young to play. The older children years ago had declared us to be incompetent and unfit to participate. Now, we knew that we were ready. The bravest of us stepped forward to claim the position of team captain. There was at first the expected silence and eye rolling by our seniors. They whispered amongst themselves and soon agreed to allow us to play. For the first time, we proudly began to participate in the selection of players.

Play-cousin Candy continued to be an unusual young lady. It was the custom to always pick her last no matter what the game. She was an only child who lived in a large and rambling house near the top of the hill with her mother. The most irritating tick in her multi-flawed personality was the way she whined or cried without much provocation. Incidents of pouting by Candy seemed to always occur in front of an adult witness. The witness would then promptly report the incident to Candy's mother. Her mother passed along the details to anyone who would listen. Eventually, the news reached its true destination, the offender's parents. I had long ago lost count of how many times I had been punished for being the cause of one of Candy's crying tantrums.

The Village adults placed great confidence in her ability. This was probably because her outward appearance was always immaculate. I wondered why my mother seemed to admire this strange girl with a high pitched, squeaky voice. Candy openly prided herself as being known as a good child. When she entered a room, the rest of us were paled by her disgustingly polite and over-polished manners. The only mystery regarding her was about her choice of shoes. We all wondered why she insisted on wearing what we knew to be grossly uncomfortable patent leather shoes.

Our opinion of Candy disagreed with that of our parents. We children strongly suspected she was more than a bit warped and at the least not exactly what she seemed to be on the outside.

The captain's choice of players in reality represented the true Village pecking order. As a whole we were all relentlessly competitive. Some of us would go to great lengths to claim victory. The most desirable characteristic for a player to exhibit was the desire to win in addition to the ability to consistently score. An actual win meant that the champions also held the most prized daily right to brag without mercy. Each game ended in controversy. Once the true winner was decided, the chiding of the losers began. The next day the losers would have to endure the recanting of each of their mistakes by the winners in exact detail over and over again.

Niece was a late-comer to our Village. She was from the first day the most competitive of all the girls. At the age of eleven, she moved from the inner-city to live in a comfortable multi-family dwelling in the Village with her grandmother. It was a mystery as to what type of person she had been before her abrupt and disruptive arrival. In short order, we became painfully aware that Niece was a loud and arrogant bully.

She brazenly hit the street without so much as batting an eye and demanded to be captain. She clinched her crooked teeth together, wrinkled her narrow brow and threw a fist into the air in support of her position. Most of us preferred to relent to her demands. Niece's initial victory and many more to come were won because our parents had warned us, "never fight a crazy person."

A sense of order, mutual strength and understanding always existed between us. Perhaps this was due to the fact that we numbered only 9 out of a total elementary school population of over 500. We argued and even had numerous confrontations, but we always knew we could rely on each other without question. Prior to Niece's arrival, life in the Village had been a comfortable existence. There was little need to be disruptive or confrontational.

Certain people always sat beside certain other people on the bus and some weren't allowed to sit at all. After eight years together the pecking order was firmly established. Niece was our first real challenge. She immediately disturbed the normal order of everything. The post-Niece era was represented by an increase in altercations that extended even beyond the divisive hedge. She was a Hitler-type leader with no regard for old understandings and less tolerance for members of the Village that dared to oppose her.

Candy's position in the pecking order decreased even further during the Niece era. Countless times Niece descended on Candy and actually severely flogged her while Candy desperately tried to escape her grasp. The only members of the Village that seemed to be able to control Niece were the male members of her family and her short but strong-willed grandmother.

The three-story multi-family dwelling in which Niece lived occupied a crowded lot at the bottom of the street in the middle of the Village. There were three generations of permanent kin and an endless string of visiting relatives that flocked and roosted within the walls of the home. Most of the younger members of the household were brother-cousins. The wise matriarch capitalized on the existence of an ample supply of free-labor by utilizing the talents of the robust young men. Therefore, the outside of the house always had a new coat of paint every spring. The cement steps that rose from the street to their front door were kept clean and in good condition by her unwilling workforce.

The brother-cousins were athletic, strong and tall. One brother-cousin also excelled as a student. He was known for his gentle nature, dark and smooth good looks. The youngest of the kin had a reputation for being overtly arrogant. Another brother-cousin was seen mostly on the weekends. He lived with his parents in the inner-city and wore all the latest styles and his clothes fit just right. This brother-cousin was the Village children's first example of how to conduct yourself as you try to live a "cool" life. All the brother-cousins except the youngest were older than Niece. Universally, and to the dismay of Niece they did not tolerate her never-ceasing attempts at manipulation.

As we moved into our teens, Niece was the first to smoke and she encouraged the use of a more potent level of profanity. She boldly ventured into other areas of the city and made friends and enemies by the truckload. Niece knew where the parties were and to which event a thirteen year old might be welcomed. We'd tell our parents we were off to the local movie but instead we usually followed Niece. It was foolish and stupid to roam outside your section of the city. If it was discovered that you did not actually live in the neighborhood in which the party was being held, it was not uncommon to be confronted. Often you did not escape without some sort of physical confrontation.

I became a Niece follower in order to remain healthy and to qualify for fewer sessions of Niece persecution. On one occasion, Niece and her followers- including me - ventured into a very rough neighborhood to attend a soirée. I had to admit that this party was a real winner because there seemed to be a great many unattached young men. Everything for an hour or so proceeded smoothly. It was then that we made our first mistake. We decided to separate and try to mingle with the crowd.

Suddenly, I heard Niece's bullhorn voice thunder, "That's right! I'm from the other side of town, fuck you!" The crowd began to rumble and move towards Niece. A cold chill ran down my spine. I desperately tried to weigh all my options. At first glance, it appeared I had only one escape route. I started to move towards it.

Niece continued to rant in a louder and louder voice. At this point, the crowd separated long enough for me to see her and another follower standing in front of one of the girls who must have lived in the community. Niece's big mouth and baseless threats in no way caused the young woman a moment of hesitation. She suddenly flashed a long knife. One of Niece's true followers bravely stepped forward to defend her heroine. The follower was promptly slashed on her right arm while a grossly outnumbered Niece continued to rant and rave.

I realized that this was my opportunity to step up to the line. A girl confronted me on my way to the only door by asking, "Didn't you come in with them?" I found exactly how much allegiance I had for Niece because, like Peter in the Bible, I denied them over and over again.

The story of the confrontation spread quickly in the Village. Niece's huge family received a summons to report to the hospital. There they found her battered and beaten. The follower with the cut on her arm was stitched and consoled. Her mother was standing over her. At least every five minutes she had to be restrained from grabbing her daughter by her hospital gown as she repeatedly threatened to kill her.

I had made it home without a scratch or regret. My parents were informed through the Village grapevine that I too had been at the party. I could see that they were profoundly disappointed when they confronted me. They asked me to tell them exactly what happened. After telling them the story of my escape, the response from my mother absolutely floored me. She calmly said, "It's better to flee and survive to fight another day."

Niece maintained her domineering behavior according to the stories told by those who cared to follow her progress over the years.

The opportunity to share our personal growth helped to mold each of us. I experienced with these complex personalities almost every emotion and fear imaginable for over fourteen years. Sometimes, when I behave like a pouting Candy, I have to face the truth that she was a fine example of how to escape responsibility. When confronted by miserable personal treatment, I admit to sometimes going as far as assuming a Niece posture to resist persecution.

Our childhood relationships heavily influence exactly what type of people we finally became. We pushed, shoved, loved, hated and observed each other without realizing the real power in what we were doing. Witnessing the failures and victories of my friends in the Village provided me with critical insight and courage. Realistically, I have to give them as much credit as my parents for helping me to be the individual I am today.

CHAPTER 25 -- BEAUTY, CHANGE AND FEAR

The expectations for a fabulous football season soared along with a hope for an early Thanksgiving holiday break. We were now old enough to be in our first year of high school. Each day's bus ride extended an additional half hour in both directions. We found our schedules crowded and often unmanageable. For the first time the opportunity seemed to be available to join organizations that offered exposure to topics that we actually found interesting. Coupled with this was the welcomed independence and challenge offered by the novelty of having to report to a different classroom for each subject.

The school had less than 20 Afro-American students. This was despite the fact that the total population of the facility was well over 2000. Some things did not change. Once again the Village children could not directly relate to any member of the predominately Caucasian faculty or staff. The massive and imposing building provided a sanitary and vacant environment that did not in any way resemble the small and cozy junior high school which had been a haven for the previous two years. A twisting and elevated driveway approach confronted the congested bus each morning. This always required the driver to downshift desperately in order to successfully ascend the hill.

Each day in the hollow hallways the voices mingled in an attempt to warm the endless space within each corridor. The classrooms were crowded and most had a gradually elevated architecture that provided a space at the base for the instructor and 5 tiers at different levels in front of this space for the rows of desks. A no-nonsense, zero-tolerance attitude regarding anything that could be viewed as offensive behavior prevailed and was strictly enforced. Hall passes were required to leave the classroom and monitors would send any offender immediately to the office. Incidents of school violence simply did not exist. The true purpose for the vigilance of the administration was to provide structure and order. Any infraction that disturbed the supervised flow of day-to-day operations would immediately be recognized and brought to an abrupt end. Chaos did not stand a change to take hold in this high school environment.

Every club and organization held a recruiting meeting that was announced on billboards throughout the school at the beginning of the session. Participation in sports by the Village children was encouraged. The white athletic coaching staff recognized our athletic prowess. Intellectual clubs could not prevent an ethnically different applicant from joining. Exceptions were taken however during the elections for positions of importance such as class officers. We rarely received even a nomination. Large organizations like the band welcomed any applicant that could successfully hoist an instrument and walk to the beat of the percussion section. I traded my violin for a French horn and joined the band.

For the most part, the Village girls were very attractive. This fact did not help us make the squads of either the cheerleaders or the majorettes. It was at this time that the gauntlet was cast and the challenge first offered to us to adhere to our personal standards in order to gauge beauty. Some of us were crushed when we discovered that our blossoming attributes were viewed by many of our classmates as obtuse, comical and downright ugly.

A privileged few of the students at this school lived in an area of town that was even more affluent than the neighborhood. They were extremely well-to-do and wore only the latest fashions made of the finest fabrics. Inter-white prejudice was proving to be a very flexible entity. It quickly modified to include this privileged few. They were immediately placed into the top caste of a new social order. Position within this system was based almost solely upon opulence. Suddenly, our middle-classed Caucasian peers of the neighborhood, who were the former holders of the honor of being at the top round of the social tier, found themselves forced to make a downward adjustment. No longer did they easily win the elections or become team captains. Now, they found themselves having to struggle just to be noticed by not only their peers but many members of the faculty. Naturally, we didn't have to make even one small change to prepare for the new social order. Our position was written somewhere in stone and guaranteed to be where it always was, at the very bottom.

The administration of frequent placement tests and the related curriculum were designed to separate the student population into two groups. The theory was that the entire process eventually would position us into one of these groups based on whether or not we had aspirations and the ability to attend college. Generally, the two groups rarely found any reason to mingle. The majority of the student body was on the fast track to college. The few students who had vocational technical interests found themselves isolated and unwelcome.

Football, basketball and track events always attracted a large turnout from the community. Pride in the school was shared and expected for many reasons. Above all, we had the reputation to be one of only three institutions that promoted superior academic excellence in the greater Pittsburgh area. Our school also was the home of several very powerful athletic squads. However, all this goodness and consistent over achievement did not stop racial slurs from freely floating around the school. The only time we demonstrated a united front was in front of an opposing team.

An awareness of the existence of Martin Luther King, Jr. and Malcolm X came primarily from the television set or was found in popular periodicals and magazines. This is not hard to understand when it is explained that as far as the science, math and literature textbooks of this era were concerned, there was clearly only one significant contribution to society by an Afro-American worth mentioning. A degree of modest tribute was given to George Washington Carver. He was hailed as being the master of the peanut and an educator of colored people. Yet, we weren't told of even one of the many accomplishments of the alumni of the institution he founded in Tuskegee, Alabama.

Pennsylvania state history emphasized its proud membership in the Union and the fact that the civil war was fought to free the slaves. Slavery was explained as being an instrument used by the greedy South to supply a free workforce to harvest their chief crop of cotton. Once again, many facts were omitted. The institution of slavery and how it had been a prosperous European industry for almost a century was not addressed in any way.

On the other hand, our history books did clearly provide us with at least two very real enemies: Nazi Germany and Communist Red Russia. We were warned that they were both lined up against us. An attack was imminent and it would probably be launched from somewhere in Cuba or South America. Above all, the admonishment was repeated over and over again that they were plotting everyday to overrun our fair minded, equality based nation.

The development of the African continent was almost completely ignored. This promoted and protected Black ignorance even extended into shielding us from vital information associated with prominent world leaders of any color other than white. We were not told about apartheid in South Africa. The only holocaust that was worth mentioning in world history was that of the Jews by the Germans during WWII. The gross lack of knowledge of the value of the black experience and the associated fear of it as being an unknown entity created a quiet environment with a potentially violent undercurrent.

The day everything changed started out as a typical sunny and bright morning in late November. A

Thanksgiving break was scheduled to kick off the following week. Everyone was excited about the many events that were planned for after school and the weekend. The bell rang in the hallway to mark the beginning of first period. We were about to enter a period of quiet -- in many ways before the storm --- that would result in a new America.

Lunch was staggered in order to accommodate the large student body. We were assigned by class to eat within a time slot between 11:00 a.m. and 12:30 a.m. Exactly when you ate depended upon into which group you were assigned. I was scheduled for the second shift. When I reached the cafeteria door, there was a group of teachers directing our group to immediately report to our homerooms. Because the school was so large, most of the student body and faculty were still in the hallways making our way to or from the cafeteria.

Suddenly, over the PA the principal informed us that President Kennedy had been shot. I tried hard to hear where all this was happening. All around me the murmuring and weeping became so loud that I could only make out that he was somewhere in Texas. It was as if an invisible hammer had fallen on the very heart of our school. The teachers were able to restore order, and after several long minutes the outward displays of shock were replaced with an uneasy silence.

A short year before we had survived the Cuban Missile Crisis. Prior to that, we spent a solid eight years training for the inevitable third world war. We did our part by participating in drills that foolishly required us to hide under our desks in elementary school to avoid radiation poisoning. Civil studies and World History lead us to believe that the United States was a nation that felt itself to be strong and prepared for any emergency. November 22, 1963 was to be the day that Soviet Premier Nikita Khrushchev's dream would come true without him having to lift a finger. Every vital service and industrial facility in America stood still for almost thirty minutes awaiting an update on the condition of our President.

President John F. Kennedy was truly a man of the people. Amazingly, he was considered to be worthy of this title even during his lifetime. The reason for his popularity was simple. He offered hope and a sense of well-being to the common American. The press cautiously and selectively conducted their coverage of him within certain guidelines. The general public was not made aware of his sordid secrets. Even his critics admired his tall lean physique, his beautiful children and fashionable wife. He was a stately figure and appeared to be a true humanitarian. The Negro community adored him because he had launched a serious effort in the South that was designed to eventually break the back of discrimination.

The minutes ticked by slowly and as a class we sat in silence waiting for the next announcement. The PA buzzed and the familiar voice of Walter Cronkite was heard from a radio or TV source. Despite the static and cracking of the PA system, Cronkite's always strong voice now sounded quiet and filled with emotion. The President had been pronounced dead at Parkland Hospital.

I was too shocked to cry. I simply couldn't believe the whole thing was real. Most of our teachers unsuccessfully tried to fight back the tears. Cronkite's announcement was followed immediately by a call for the teachers to report to the auditorium. That day it wasn't necessary for them to warn the students to be still while they were gone. We weren't even talking to one another. It was the first time in my life that I just wanted everything to slow down. School was immediately dismissed and the entire student body loaded onto buses in a numb and speechless state of shock and disbelief.

It was a death that left our parents immersed in a communal, unfamiliar and paralyzing type of grief. Many of them were unable or unwilling to return to work for several days. Television became the only thing that was of interest to the public. For the first time in history, TV made it possible to see first hand the minute to minute progress of a traumatizing situation. That evening a horrified and shocked populous watched while Jackie Kennedy in a blood-stained pink suit accompanied the body of her husband back to Washington. We barely had time to begin the grief process when the very next day the supposed assassin was himself gunned down as a national TV audience continued to watch in disbelieve. For a short period, that seemed like it would last forever, the heart and soul of America crumbled. The horror continued and it brought little comfort that it was all being meticulously documented on a flickering black and white screen by the powerful media organizations.

This was the first in a series of unaccounted for, unexplained deaths. The entire decade was soon to be perverted and twisted. We, as a nation, slowly grew to be much too comfortable with the "Special Announcements" on TV that marked the passing of one more national hero.

History was to deal kindly with Kennedy. He is often described as a dreamer who had the courage to go against the grain of political society. One immediate and unsettling effect of his untimely death was that it seemed for a while even the clocks stopped ticking. This horrible and catastrophic event released waves of gut rendering depression, suspicion and confusion that would ebb and resurface even into a new century.

There was a display of flags and even exchanges of heartfelt discussions at the grocery stores in our community. Members of the Village and neighborhood shared their disbelief in muted tones. The major question asked by all the experts at that time was a simple, "Why?" Politicians and commentators in tears could not provide an answer. The intense level of grief was unrelenting. Soon, a fear of the demise of the entire nation began to be echoed by members of the press.

As we watched, we were at first in a state of shock and then frightened as the killing and confusion escalated. At some point, a hard shell began to cover our hearts. We didn't realize that this conditioning to absorb terror and fear on TV would one day leave us unable to respond normally to death and grief. The nation did not parish. However, it was forever changed.

President Kennedy's death marked a beginning of the desensitizing of America. From that point forward, a hunger developed in the soul of a nation that could be satisfied only by the frequent application of fear and destruction. Violent acts in all shapes and forms became commonplace. We had to accept the fact that even in this country these kinds of assaults could happen again, at any time and for absolutely no logical reason.

CHAPTER 26 -- POVERTY IN THE SUBURBS

The months that followed the death of President Kennedy, his assassin and the associated death of a strange and corrupt Texas businessman with questionable connections produced very little change in the manner in which business was conducted between the Village and the neighborhood. The main thoroughfare at the edge of the neighborhood continued to contain thriving businesses that were not owned, operated or staffed for the most part by members of the Village.

The family practitioner generously made discounted, occasional house calls from his dingy and depressing office on the second floor above a card shop. There he treated primarily the basic head cold and other common maladies. He worked long hours and it's doubtful that he had enough money or the time to enjoy the sun while playing a round of golf or tennis. Therefore, his skin was very white, as was that of the resident dentist. They both served all members of the diverse community. The two of them seemed to operate their businesses without prejudice or extreme profit. The irony was that if your illness became serious and you happened to pass away, the funeral homes and graveyards within a range of four miles of the Village only accepted Caucasian clients.

Living below the edge of poverty as an American Negro did not guarantee that you could acquire adequate healthcare. The state of Pennsylvania had many clinics in the counties. The resources of these institutions could be combined with benefits from the federal government to assure minimal coverage for a constituent as long as the citizen did not own property. Property owners who literally lived from paycheck to paycheck did not qualify for any level of compensation. Instead, they found themselves excluded and denied much needed medical assistance. Unfortunately, the propertied poor also avoided frequent necessary checkups and consultations. The family practitioner realized the desperate and dangerous situation imposed by the bureaucratic structure. He made every effort he could to persuade his colleagues to accept referrals from the ranks of the working poor Village members.

Most of the fathers in the Village held jobs that required back-braking labor that often had to be performed in life-threatening conditions. The average male in the Village could not expect to live beyond the age of 45. Many of them had extra-curricular activities that probably only shortened their life expectancy. "Black male machismo" required them to subscribe to certain perverse activities that too often resulted in the creation of several "outside children." A hunger to satisfy sexual fantasies in which they consummated unions with countless willing women was combined with the over-consumption of alcohol on a daily basis.

It was not necessary for them to lie to their spouses. After all, the entire situation was treated by the rest of the Village as unfortunate, regrettable but expected.

There were instances of spousal abuse usually performed by intoxicated husbands that required police intervention. An eruption was more likely to occur following the return to the fold by a black macho father who had left the majority of his paycheck in the hands of the other woman. The behavior of these few men that subscribed to a violence-prone existence was too often reflected in the bruised and battered faces of their wives. These twisted characters were not in the majority but they had a damaging and lasting influence on some of the Village children.

In the '60s a teenage pregnancy was not an uncommon occurrence. The expenses related to the bearing of illegitimate children in a land-owning, poor family was often the exclusive responsibility of the parents' of the young mother. It was also not atypical for the shocked teenage father to suddenly find himself the target of a shotgun-wedding. Liaisons of this nature tended to be short and marked by a type of violence that did not prevent the creation of even more children. Birth control methods that were somewhat reliable did exist but the new subscribers to the black male machismo lifestyle often refused to utilize any type of protection. The teenage father followed in the footsteps of his abusive father, and the teenage mother accepted a life without truth and commitment. Reluctantly, for a brief period of time, it seemed the children of the village were destined to imitate their parents. This was especially true for the generation composed of our older brothers and sisters. Fortunately, the adults of the Village became more determined to break the mold after we appeared on the scene.

Teenage pregnancy was not an exclusive problem of the Village. An indication that a girl was pregnant was that she suddenly was absent from school. Unexplained absences were also not uncommon within the ranks of the girls of the neighborhood. The luxury of school attendance was prohibited for the mother by the Board of Education and she would have to finish high school in a special education environment. Absolutely no special consideration was given as to her grade point average or extra-curricular commitments. The father of the child had the option to remain in school and it was possible for him to continue his life without interruption.

CHAPTER 27 -- HAROLD AND THE WELFARE SYSTEM

Harold was a tall and rather plump young man who appeared to have few aspirations. The years of his childhood in the Village were full of male-bonding experiences. Like his father, he loved the ladies. Age 16 found Harold stimulated by an exciting world full of conked-hair, acappella-singing-on-the-corner sessions, motorcycle and Chevy collecting and the birth of rock-n-roll. His first taste of adulthood came in the arms of a girl of the Village and the result was the creation of their first child. The mother of the baby was immediately dismissed from school and Harold, at the insistence of his strong mother, married to provide an honorable last name for the baby. Harold had never held a job and his behavior indicated from the very beginning that he considered himself a victim in a situation that was really not his fault.

The marriage of Harold's parents had survived many years in which his father would come home so intoxicated that he was barely able to negotiate the stairwell that ascended to their house. Harold was a highly verbal member of a group of young men that stood under the street lights in the early summer evenings to brag about their latest conquests.

The young couple was able to finally move into a rundown house at the top of the street in the Village. The old tar paper covered residence had gaping holes in almost every wall. Weekends continued to be special for Harold. He had somehow found a ridiculously low-paying job that barely provided enough money to cover the rent. His bride was left home in front of a new TV that had been a wedding present while Harold met his social obligations.

Numerous times his life seemed to wander into very dangerous waters. Shortly after the birth of their first child a second was on the way. His choice of women tended to be ill-fated. One woman reportedly picked him up and threw him head-first through a plate glass window of a barber shop. Another delivered several cuts to his body that could have easily killed him. The birth of the babies, Harold's hospital stays due to the injuries inflicted on him by his other girlfriends and the medical expenses for his growing family were all taken on for the most part by Harold's family. The couple remained in the drafty and damp house, and the production line of children moved forward with the delivery of their third and final child.

A change had come over Harold and his new bride that was reflected in their deteriorating personal appearances. Pre-marriage Harold loved glistening starched shirts, leather jackets, and the company of his peers. He'd spent every spare penny he could to purchase the best lye-based formula that would assure that his hair was konked just right. He enjoyed the benefits of a gleaming motorcycle that he religiously cleaned and polished. School tended to be a thing he did because it was expected. The future did not exist for him as a concern because of his obsessive interests in the present.

Harold's wife before the marriage had been shy, of average build and unimposing. She possessed an appreciation for the benefits of education and was known to verbalize her aspirations to become a nurse. The majority of pre-marital weekends were spent taking long walks with her friends or riding the streetcar to downtown Pittsburgh for a shopping spree. There were many children in her family and also a history of alcohol abuse. The things that were important to Harold did not even register as a glitch on her radar screen.

Post-marital Harold was obese and without most of his prized possessions. His hair had to be cut completely off after a mishap with a cheap homemade conking concoction that burned his scalp almost to the bone. His wife's weight soared until she reached over 300 pounds. They were bloated and unrecognizable. Both did not complete their high school educations. Soon, they found their lives filled with physical confrontations, little money, mounting bills and a related sense of defeat. Formerly proud Harold rode the streetcar and borrowed money from every relative. Their existence was plagued by what they started to call bad luck and desperation. A move to the inner-city projects was viewed as a step up in society after the broken down house at the top of the street in the Village was condemned.

The couple desperately tried to stay together even though Harold repeatedly moved in and out of their shared housing. Their children naturally loved both parents and bravely endured session after session of intense screaming, crying and fighting. In many ways, Harold took the frequently intoxicated example set by his father to an even lower depth of debauchery.

In the background and never far from the side of Harold and his wife were their families. They continued to provide not only money but emotional support throughout the tumultuous marriage. Numerous times the children's need for clothing and food became very expensive and critical. The young family found itself at the doors of the federal welfare system for this reason after nearly three years of marriage.

The marriage was put to the final test once they accepted the terms necessary to move within the walls of the public housing system. Harold's meager income did not prevent them from qualifying for housing but it did disqualify them for assistance in other areas. He could not meet the challenge to provide medical care, food and clothing for his family without support from the welfare system. A decision was soon made that would change everything despite any of Harold's or his wife's considerations to form a united future.

The rules that determined qualifications for support were designed to only be applicable to one parent families. An employed, legal father's presence in the home could be considered grounds for termination of all services. The sliding scale at the bottom of society contained only a few notches to determine eligibility. Adherence to the regulations was monitored by a staff of case workers who were authorized to make unannounced visits to assure the separated or divorced couple remained apart. Harold's efforts to find a better job no longer mattered. The couple agreed it was best for the children that they separate.

The young mother set her mind to successfully raising the children. Harold simply packed his clothes and moved out. After finally getting a decent job, he moved to another state. The children grew up fatherless in the inner city. Unfortunately their lives often mirrored that of their parents.

In the case of this young family it is possible that theologians would credit their inability to escape a damaging cycle that included numerous illegitimate births, spousal abuse and poverty as an inherent situation known formally as, "the sin of the father." Sociologists have made numerous attempts to address "black male machismo" but seem at a loss to explain why a race of oppressed people seem to condone and support in song and verse the skill of a man to make a whore out of a woman in order to repeatedly satisfy his needs.

Society after the death of Kennedy began to crumble. The pieces fell on the heads of people like Harold and his family who found themselves at the bottom. The decay continued without much protest or formal recognition. America was now one of many similar societies in which the leaders seem to pride themselves in their unique ability to design biased and destructive institutions.

The Village, with limited resources, tried to accommodate Harold. All this was done despite the lack of support from the neighborhood. In fact, a few of their shops had cut back their hours of operation because of the growing level of uncertainty. American businesses were finding out that insecure customers tend to buy a lot less. They also seemed to be having their own very personal problems. The number of our white fellow classmates that suddenly dropped out of school also seemed to be increasing. We, the next generation took note of one disturbing and indisputable fact. The adults were not in control of the serious and shared problems that were affecting the very lives of their children on both sides of the divisive bush. The inability to hold a worthwhile conversation that would effectively address these issues was now a threat to the health and survival of every family in the area.

CHAPTER 28 -- SEPARATION

Some people actually seem to know exactly when they are going to die. In most cases they do all they can to prepare their family. Sometimes, they even start to take steps to dispense with treasured assets. It is also common for them to inform anyone who will listen in such a way that the hearer becomes convinced there is truth in their dire declaration. The result of the unloading of information seems to provide them with a feeling of peace and contentment. Conversely, the acquired statement of mortality has the ability to fill the listener with a watchful sense of dread and fear.

Health complications began a slow process that would eventually overtake my mother during the late spring of 1962. Her once crowded schedule, that included twelve hours of work for the rich German and trips to the inner city to visit relatives or beloved churches, gradually had to be altered and finally abandoned. The local practitioner prescribed a blood thinner and advised her that there could be psychological side effects. An ulcer formed on the calf of her left leg and behind it a blood clot began to maliciously develop. It was at this time that she tearfully announced, "I know I won't live much longer. It's God's plan and I'm alright with that."

The information terrified both me and my father. Treatments at the local VA hospital for the bone cancer that he'd contracted had been underway the past three years. He was able to remain at home only because of the diligent care he'd received from my mother. Periodically, he had to be hospitalized. This required my mother to undertake an extensive trip across town to a treatment center that sat at the apex of a panoramic hill. By now, streetcars no longer were the primary mode of transportation. They had been replaced with diesel fuel burning buses. These vehicles spouted harsh smelling fumes that filled the streets of downtown Pittsburgh with clouds of thick, noxious, black and greasy soot.

The day long trip to the treatment center required making two bus transfers. This was followed by an almost mile long walk from the bus stop up a winding and elevated driveway approach to finally reach the facility. Money to pay for a taxicab from the Village to the hospital had to be found after the condition of my mother's leg began to rapidly deteriorate.

Finances in the household were suffering at this point because of the inability of my mother to work at either her regular legitimate job or the one she'd created by carrying numbers. The overwhelming burden of debt, unending personal responsibilities and numerous chemical side effects of medication caused her to become openly desperate and extremely tired. As justification for her soon-to-come demise she offered, "God Himself knows I am tired."

After making this bone chilling announcement, she calmly added that she had been looking for a safe place for me to live. The target family for my placement was actually a distant cousin, his wife and young daughter who lived on the North Side of town in a very attractive home. I remembered that the husband appeared to be a kind man that often offered my mother rides to the VA hospital. He volunteered to provide maintenance to the crumbling stairwell. My father was now so weak that the most he could do was to take an occasional walk around the parameter of the crooked house in the gully. This cousin often brought hot meals to our house that his wife had prepared. For the past six months, he seemed to be the only relative my mother could turn to now that her life was literally falling apart.

This became the first time in my life that I felt powerless to change or improve anything or to help anybody. I was so stunned by the entire situation that I couldn't find the strength to even protest. I'd always tried to be an obedient daughter. My grades were good in school, but I realized quickly that there was absolutely nothing I could do except prepare to begin a new life away from the two people that meant the world to me. When school was dismissed for the summer I packed my clothes in boxes as my mother, with tears streaming down her face, looked on from the doorway.

The cousin, his wife and daughter promptly arrived at a previously agreed upon time. After consoling my mother and hugging her and my father, they promised to care for me as if I were one of their own. I had no idea what to say or how to act. My mother seemed to sense that I was overwhelmed and simply assured me that, "Everything's going to be alright." Familiar sights of the Village and the maple and oak lined streets of the neighborhood raced by the car window as I sat in the back seat of my new caretakers light blue Ford coupe.

We arrived at their neat frame home during the middle of a sunny and bright day. Their North Side neighborhood contained houses that were at the most only 5 feet apart with sidewalks and short spans of stairwells that lead to the front door of each dwelling. I would now be living even closer to downtown Pittsburgh. The plan was that I should return to the same high school I had been attending in order to provide some sort of stability. Over the next few weeks, I tried to keep my new room clean and offered to do housework. It was unusual to have to adjust to the needs of a sibling. I made a special effort to relate to and play with their 4 year old daughter. In my heart I felt abandoned. Most of the time, I sat alone reading on the short front stoop to the house or just stared at the wall in my light blue, cheerful new bedroom.

One day, after I had been with the family for almost three weeks, the cousin summoned me to the bottom of the steps of the two storied dwelling. His wife had taken the baby and gone to visit a relative. He indicated that I should follow him because he had something special to show me. I was told to go ahead of him up the steps while behind me he kept telling me how much I was going to enjoy his surprise. I paused in the hallway at the top of the stairs, and he took me by the arm and led me towards his bedroom. Never in the history of my visits to the homes of my friends in the Village had I ever been permitted to enter the bedroom of any of their parents. In fact, the doors to their bedrooms had always been closed. An alarm within me sounded. Unfortunately, this voice was muffled by the knowledge that my wise mother trusted this man. I slowed my steps and he must have felt my reluctance. At this point, he left me and went into the room and picked up an envelope that was lying on the dresser.

He again assured me that it was alright to come in. For some reason, I could not get myself to obey his command. I stood waiting outside the bedroom. He began to approach me while opening the envelope. "Look at these, they're really something. I bet you'd like to do some of this, wouldn't you?"

He held the pictures proudly in his hand and rotated them in front of me one after another. They were vivid shots of nude men and women having all types of sex and close-ups of the genital areas of both a man and a woman. It was clear now that I was in danger and without saying a single word I turned and went back down the stairs. I looked at the front door and realized that I could easily walk the four miles back to the Village. Yet the memory of my promise to make this situation work to my mother combined with her delicate health gave me strength enough to believe that I could somehow stay out of the lecherous cousin's grasp and survive whatever hell he planned for me.

The cousin did not follow me down the steps. It seemed that over the next week he made extra efforts to avoid me. His wife never had much to say most of the time. Since he was now also silent, the house was eerily quiet. I tried to fill my days by reading and I purposefully stayed on the first floor every evening from the time I got up until the couple had settled into bed for the night. It was a miserable situation, but I refused to complain and never mentioned anything to my mother during our daily phone conversations.

One day an unexpected knock was heard at the door. The shy wife-cousin opened it and to our surprise there stood my mother. The two women and I went into the kitchen. During the course of the conversation, my mother calmly explained to her that she simply missed me far more than she'd ever imagined. It was then that she turned to me and told me to pack my clothes because I would be leaving. The wife-cousin protested to no avail. Soon, I found myself beside my mother in a taxi on my way back to the safety of the Village. She asked if I'd had a good time. I was so grateful to see her that all I could do was respond with a lump in my throat, "yes ma'am." I knew she had once again saved me. I also realized that it wasn't necessary to tell her the bad thing that had happened. It is possible that the cousin feared that I had confided in my mother. He rarely made appearances at our crooked house from that day forward.

The upcoming twelve months were full of repeated trips to physicians. I accompanied my mother as her leg continued to swell to the point that it looked like a log of wood. The inflamed quarter-sized ulcer behind her right knee constantly required cleansing. No matter how hard we tried, the pus continued to run from the wound despite the application of prescribed topical ointments and oral medications. We desperately needed money and she tried to continue to work at least one day a week. Soon, the pain and drugs wore down her determination. She was forced to stay in bed.

This was to be a last ditch effort to heal the inflamed open wound.

She became dependent upon me for many of the household tasks. At the age of fifteen, I was left to manage most of my personal decisions. I had developed a more than mild crush on one of the members of the track team. For a brief period of time he shared my interest. We walked hand in hand through the snow covered streets of both the Village and neighborhood. On two occasions, he even visited me at my home. The tall, handsome first love of my life slow danced and explored nearly every inch of my young body in the living room beneath her bedroom floor as my mother watched TV and nursed her injured leg.

He was chocolate brown, tall muscular and extremely popular with an intoxicating smell based on Aqua Velva after shave. Our mutual attraction, for him, lasted only three weeks. During that time, I managed to embarrass myself by performing with him a scorching slow dance at a basement party. We both lost track of where we were and before the end of James Brown's "Bewildered" stroked and grinned our way into the snack table and managed to fall together into a huge bowl of potato chips.

We fondled each other with an urgency that is only possible to experience in youth. We were never left alone long enough to complete the act. I began to suspect that my mother possessed a second sense for my situation. Whenever things were about to get too heated she would suddenly call for me. After hearing her voice, he became noticeably uncomfortable. Generally, and within only a few minutes, he found it easy to rearrange his pants, make some lame excuse and leave.

Shortly after the end of my three week romance, I noticed that my mother's health had greatly deteriorated. There were times she was barely able to contain herself from crying or becoming inconsolably angry. Most of the day, she walked the floor in an old bathrobe while desperately praying for deliverance from the bills and worry. The heat of the summer and a restricted life inside a sweltering airless house was made almost intolerable as she tried to care for an ulcerated leg that was always agonizingly painful, inflamed and on the brink of infection. She had saved me and now there was nothing I could do or say to even ease her torment.

One morning I found her in the kitchen where she'd remained during the entire night because the pain in her leg would not let her sleep. My father and I had witnessed the mood swings and we'd found the best thing to do was to try to simply avoid her until the pain subsided. But this morning she would have none of this behavior. She insisted that I stand still and listen or she'd thrash me until I got some sense into my head. She spoke of things I could not understand and suddenly accused me of not cooperating. I knew better than to argue and avoided eye contact so as not to further upset her. This also failed and with only a verbal warning of less than two words she pushed me towards the stairwell. Hatred and doubt poured out of her mouth and she began to beat me with her bare hands. It was obvious that she was having this fight with someone else because the things she accused me of were in no way relevant to me.

The blows were painful and they continued until I finally lost my balance and fell face-down onto the stairwell. Suddenly, I realized I had to put an end to it. I grabbed her arm and flipped her over beneath me while begging her to stop and look at me. She tried to free herself and violently demanded that I get off her. I released my hold and quickly darted for the door. I knew I couldn't stop for fear that she would get her trusty .357 and put an end to me right then and there. As I ran from the house, I could hear her enraged threats. "I'm going to call the damn cops on your smart ass! Let them deal with you!"

I sat patiently outside the crooked house near the edge of the weed infested garden. An officer arrived within the hour and he finally succeeded in calming down my mother. I was asked if I thought the whole thing could be worked out. He told me if I'd behave my mother was willing to allow me back in the home. At this time I was barely 15, but I knew my time in the gully was over.

The officer warned me of what awaited me. He said I'd become a ward of the state and have to spend time in juvenile court. My mother stood in the doorway and I refused to reenter the house. I was taken away in handcuffs and deposited inside a cell in the juvenile court detention facility. My day before the judge came and in front of my mother he indicated that I could still return home. I looked at my mother's pain filled eyes and knew in my heart that going back with her was not the right thing for either one of us.

After a few more weeks of detention, I was placed in a group home. I was only able to return to the Village one time for a short visit before my mother died. On that day I decided to walk instead of catching the bus since the group home was within two miles of the Village. I received some comfort as the familiar, chilly fall breeze wrapped around me. Occasionally, a leaf from one of the trees that had witnessed my passing over the years fell on the ground in front of me. In a period of less than two months my life had completely changed. On the other hand, the stores and homes of the neighborhood remained remote and constant. I did not feel a sense of regret or a desire to be a part of the changeless community. I no longer felt at home.

CHAPTER 29 -- A LOVELESS EXISTENCE

The detention at the juvenile facility did provide a bit of a respite. I used the month of incarceration to recover from the resentment I had begun to develop towards my foster parents. The guards initially warned me to keep to myself to avoid any possibility of conflict with the other prisoners. I was repeatedly questioned by them and by my counselor as to how I could ever allow myself to get into such trouble considering my strong academic performance and community involvement. They were amazed to discover that I was a long-time candy-stripper volunteer at the hospital and a member of an award winning high school band. I received almost constant encouragement to reconcile with my parents if it was at all possible.

After declining my mother's invitation to return to the Village, "as long as you behave" I didn't feel an ounce of regret. I could not see anyway in which I could behave any better. She had become emotionally unstable and prone to outbreaks of uncontrollable anger since the doctor felt it necessary to prescribe an anti-coagulating medication to treat an open ulcer on her leg. I didn't fear for my life. Instead, I had grown to feel emotionally drained by the entire hopeless situation. The terminal illness of my father, more frequent disruptive home visits by the prodigal daughter and volatile and uncertain mental state of my mother became a burden I could no longer bear.

At the direction of the judge I was sentenced to live in Termon Avenue Home and given permission to visit the Village and my parents only once per month for the first ninety days. The guards had grown to be frustrated by my behavior. It was obvious that they considered me to be selfish and inconsiderate. When I left the detention facility, they informed me that I "would be back" because girls like me always found a way to stay in trouble. I heard them but I knew better than to accept what they were saying. It was at this time that I began to feel empowered. Somehow, I knew that I had the strength to take care of myself. Above all, I realized that I was completely alone and responsible for my own success or failure. It was time to apply all the lessons I had learned while growing up in the Village.

Termon Avenue Home was an all-girl facility for juvenile delinquents located between the North Side and the city of Pittsburgh. The residents mostly came from the inner city. Most of them had been involved in non-violent acts ranging from prostitution to illegal drug use and distribution. My juvenile court counselor advised me that I was allowing myself to be placed into a dangerous situation. She felt I would in no way have the emotional tools to adjust and even tried to arrange a compromise to permit me to return home at the last moment. My mother was open to the idea. I flatly refused.

"You will be staying on the second floor and lights out is always 8:30. You will be assigned chores which must be done or you will not earn your allowance. We have enrolled you in Allegheny High School on the North Side and all your things from your mother are in the closet at the foot of the stairs. We expect you to ride the transit bus each day to and from school and late arrivals to or from school will not be tolerated." This was the beginning of a long and harsh welcome given to me by the head matron, Mrs. Chapman. She was a short, barrel shaped, bug-eyed, humorless woman who seemed to be approaching her mid-fifties. Her legs were extremely bowed and she rocked from leg to leg as she walked. Around her neck she wore a chain from which her thick glasses bobbed and weaved from huge breast to breast. In her mangled right hand she carried a massive ring of keys that rattled constantly. She was only able to ascend or descend the stairs one step at a time. Her uneven gait and rattling keys provided an advance warning of her presence.

Mrs. Chapman's major drawback was that she had a very weak voice. This proved to be a liability whenever she had to assert her authority as head matron. She practiced corporal punishment on the younger girls by liberally applying heavy swats to their rear ends with a paddle. Unfortunately, she often seemed powerless whenever she tried to discipline the older residents. It was obvious from even my first day that she feared the more mature young women in the facility.

"We expect you to do well in school due to your past academic record. Because you have been interested in school, we want to help you adjust. We're going to let you work with one of our better students, Nancy. She's very quiet. If you're smart, you can learn from her how to get along here." At this point she paused long enough to make notes in what I thought must have been my file. "Do you have any questions?"

I didn't sense a genuine interest in my well-being coming from this strange woman. Therefore, I politely nodded my head to acknowledge that I understood and declined to ask any questions.

She began to break off a piece of cake from the slice sitting on the side of her desk. I would have to grow accustomed to conversations with Mrs. Chapman with food tumbling from her mouth. She constantly snacked. I would also have to grow used to the fact that she obviously in no way wanted to be a mother figure to me or anyone in the building.

I was shown the kitchen and dining room with its many wooden tables and hard chairs. Mrs. Chapman advised me that raids on the refrigerator would not be tolerated. At this time I noticed the shiny hard wood floors, clean windows and numerous doors which I assumed were locked.

The entire facility was not a disappointment. I had expected to be living in a place with many more obvious restrictions. The huge three storied house sat on a massive lot at the end of a narrow cobblestone road. I would be allowed to freely roam the property. Above all, I was able to return to high school so that I could still meet the Village objective of attending college.

Nancy eventually found me later that day on the second floor unpacking my clothes. "Hi, I'm Nancy

and Mrs. Chapman wanted me to introduce myself."
She asked me to follow her and took me for the first
time to the third floor which seemed to be populated
mostly by the older girls. Nancy didn't have a great deal
to say beyond the initial introduction. It was obvious
that she had her own agendas. By the end of the day, I
had met most of the girls in the home. None of them
seemed to be particularly interested in establishing a
friendship.

It was now very late in the afternoon. I could
smell dinner as it was being prepared in the kitchen. I
carefully descended the shiny wooden steps and noticed
that they were dangerously slick. As I started to enter
the large sleeping area, I was taken by surprise to see a
very large girl with speckled skin brazenly rambling
through my boxes. "You got somethin' to say!" She
glared at me and started to walk towards me. "This
stupid girl thinks she can fuck with me." I knew I
couldn't run away and realized I probably didn't stand a
chance to defend myself against such a large and
formidable opponent.

Suddenly, the sound of Mrs. Chapman's uneven
gait and rattling keys could be heard in the hallway.
"Everybody get ready for dinner. Food will be on the
table in five minutes." At this point, the terrifying girl
whom I later learned was named Ora, glared at me and
began to change her direction. I was grateful when she
sat down on what must have been her bed and began to
read a magazine. We both knew someday there would
be another opportunity for a confrontation. My
experience with bullies told me that this one should
definitely be avoided.

I didn't eat much even though the food was quite
good. Instead, I sat quietly and observed my follow

residents. Some had decent table manners while others seemed to struggle to even properly use their utensils. After my juvenile court incarceration, I now knew that I had lived a sheltered life in the Village. This fact didn't help me to not feel shocked that there could be a whole set of other children that obviously hadn't been trained to even eat properly. Food fell countless times from their over-stuffed mouths onto the starched white table clothes. Several of the younger girls occasionally threw small bits of food at one another whenever they thought Mrs. Chapman was not looking. I ate in silence and observed my peers with my head bowed as their eyes examined me. Common sense told me to not let them know anything about me.

    I avoided direct eye contact while in the home. For the first two months, I only spoke on the few occasions when I was spoken to. The other girls had established groups to which they belonged. These were generally based on where they were raised within the city of Pittsburgh. I was also able to avoid the dangerous focus of Ora and the other bullies by assuming the posture of a loner. I wisely didn't even try to fit into any of the established groups for many months.

CHAPTER 30 -- THE COSTLY OBJECTIVE

The opportunity to attend a new high school was made a bit more of a challenge because I had to begin in the middle of a school year. Most of the other girls at the institution were required to attend Oliver school. It was also on the North Side and very near Allegheny High School where it was decided that I should continue. My caseworker advised me that she had selected Allegheny High because it was known to be one of the best inter-city schools. Nancy and I shared excellent academic records and above average aptitude test scores. She was permitted to attend a Catholic school. Most days she wore a required, drab-gray institutional uniform with a crisply ironed white blouse. We both stood out from the other girls for many reasons. Mrs. Chapman never had to look far to find either one of us. We both spent hours studying at different tables in the lunch room. Usually, she could be seen in the company of tons of books, instruments and other paraphernalia related to our shared collegiate ambitions. She never discussed any of her personal objectives with me. Yet, it was easy to see a sense of purpose in her consistent behavior.

My entire world was now full of new and different people and refreshing challenges. I did my required chores at the home without being threatened or punished. I also began a lifetime hobby of observing people in order to learn how to manage my own life. Many of the girls had violent tendencies. There were several very dangerous outbreaks of temper and inter-click rivalries which periodically split the home population into factions.

One set of girls was particularly dangerous because they had parents with money. The parents provided them with nice wardrobes which even included full length leather coats. Unfortunately, the affluent parents never visited or even called them on a regular basis. They always seemed to be very angry and they made no effort to hide these feelings. It was not uncommon to hear them say that they felt justified to spend as much money as they wanted on drugs and extended unauthorized holidays from the institution with their boyfriends.

They were attractive, and deceptively convincing. Mrs. Chapman seemed to have a weakness for this group of girls. The repeated acts of disobedience on their part did not result in their removal from the home even though she constantly warned the entire population that we were all just one step away from criminal incarceration. Their elite click smoked cigarettes in the building. Repeatedly, they missed attendance at school, smuggled alcohol into their third floor sleeping quarters and successfully had sexual encounters on the grounds of the institution. It was not uncommon for them to run away from the home for periods of up to a month. Mrs. Chapman appeared to hold them in special esteem and this outraged Ora and the other less attractive bullies.

Ora was suspected to be slightly retarded because she was well over seventeen and still only in the ninth grade. She made little effort to conceal a violent and destructive temper. Hardly a week would go by without an eruption on her part. The outbreaks of uncontrolled fury always resulted in broken furniture, and cuts and bruises. She was full of resentment and hatred, and it was very likely that she had severely injured someone in the past. Everyone knew Ora was a dangerous threat. If anyone deserved to be behind bars, it was her. Yet, she managed to rant, rave and beat the hell out of anyone who she thought was in her way. It was not uncommon for a group of the older girls and Mrs. Chapman to have to come to the aid of a victim who found themselves at the mercy of Ora's wrath. They would have to be torn from the grasp of a raging Ora who usually preferred to hold her screaming victim by the hair. Sometimes, she managed to even tear the hair away from their scalp in handfuls.

Nancy would spend hours talking quietly to Mrs. Chapman. This resulted in her being given a position of high regard by the administrator. I did not confide in Mrs. Chapman or anyone else in the home. For the first time, I began to doubt that there was anyone on the face of the earth that I could truly trust.

During the first year of my stay at Termon Avenue Home, two girls tried to commit suicide and several were sent off in handcuffs to other institutions because of infractions. The majority of the girls seemed to from very depressed and impoverished backgrounds. The meager outfits that they received from the state probably were the first decent clothing they had ever owned. It is also likely that the reliable three meal a day diet of the home was in fact their first exposure to consistent and good nutrition. Keeping these facts in mind, it was discouraging to see how little they appreciated their new found abundance. Many of them cried and begged constantly to be sent back home. They did this no matter how bad their circumstances had been with their uncaring parents or sometimes abusive caretakers.

I lived and prospered in the middle of chaos and began to relish the long bus rides to and from school. Sometimes, I would walk the eight mile roundtrip in order to save the bus fare for a special weekend expedition to the campus of Carnegie Mellon University on the east side of town. I would sit for hours in the libraries behind books on all sorts of subjects while imagining my college career. The dream of going to college became my sole focus and only interest. I was a dedicated student with extracurricular interests in band, theatre and gymnastics who never received invitations from fellow classmates to parties or their homes.

There was very little that could be considered normal about my first two years of high school. I chose a solitary existence and nearly missed the entire teenage experience in the process of insulating myself from what had become an unhealthy home environment. Very shortly the situation would become much worse. Eventually my objective of advancing my education would require an even greater sacrifice.

CHAPTER 31 -- BECOMING A LESSER PERSON

The second year of my residence at Termon Avenue Home was also my junior year of high school. I maintained a comfortable routine of study and weekend trips to East Liberty. There, I split my time between libraries at Carnegie Mellon and the University of Pittsburgh. Periodically, I had made short visits back to the Village to attend church. However, for the most part I had little contact with anyone from my past. I had started a new life and even found comfort in the sterile state of independence I carefully protected by avoiding inter-personal relationships.

Allegheny High was a multi-storied facility. Most of my classes that year were on the fourth floor. I had performed and tested well enough to be included in the elite college prep curriculum. The white majority of the student population lived in pockets of closely packed small frame houses within walking distance of the school. At least twenty-five percent of the students were Afro American. The majority of us maintained high academic records and a representative of our ranks could be found in every organization in the school.

The parents of my fellow students for the most part were middle-class. The majority of them had not gone to college. They participated as sponsors and encouraged the principal to recruit teachers from the graduate schools of Pitt and Carnegie. The college-centric environment at Allegheny was addictive. Honors based participation in extra-curricular activities supported my personal desire to continue my education.

"Have you ever thought about majoring in physics?" This question was asked by my physics professor who was also a post doctoral candidate at Pitt. "You really have the ability to go far in this science discipline."

"Ah, no sir, I haven't." This meek response was all I could muster.

"Why are you so surprised?" "Look, you have the grade point average. What's the problem, don't you like physics? "Maybe we can work together to try to land you a scholarship." He was the most dedicated teacher I had during my junior year and with his help most of the students had obtained passing grades in a class that was known for the number of students who usually had to take the course twice.

I was fascinated by physics but when I looked around the classroom I only saw white male faces. The teacher was also white. In the back of my mind I couldn't think of one black person I had seen during my tour of the Department of Physics at Pitt. I continued to listen to him, but somehow I lacked the courage to take advantage of his statement. In the back of my mind I knew that my mother had told me, "You can do anything you set your mind to do." But it had been a long time since I had actually been in the nurturing company of this strong woman. The sound of her words had decreased in their intensity. The new person I had become was willing to accept compromises and lacked the strength to try anything that didn't offer guaranteed success.

I looked up at him, after quickly making the decision to not follow his suggestions, and said, "Thank you, but I don't know about going to Pitt. I really want to leave Pittsburgh."

This was at best a weak and cowardly response. He looked at me in a way that let me know that he was more than a little disappointed. I tried to rationalize my behavior as being something other than what it really was, an act of self-doubt. I was truthfully terrified of the idea of attending Pitt or Carnegie Mellon. I believed I wasn't worthy or smart enough. Somewhere along the line, my confidence had been warped. The worst thing was that I did not recognize what the situation really revealed about me. I had a huge personal flaw. I refused to acknowledge that I needed another human being to help me make worthwhile decisions. I denied this at that time and for many years to come. I had no idea how much this foolish stubbornness could cost me.

The early spring of the following year I began to study for the SAT, tried out for the gymnastics team and continued to play in the school band. I was still an unknown entity to Mrs. Chapman. Above all, I had managed to escape the many conflicts and upheavals between the inmates themselves and the confrontations that seemed to be increasing between the staff and the other girls.

Some of the population of the elite third floor of the institution had graduated. A few had been caught shoplifting and one had even nearly died due to an overdose she'd acquired on one of her unofficial home visits. The head matron's elite group seemed to be falling apart at the seams.

I had witnessed unprovoked assaults on one girl who seemed especially vulnerable. Her name was Dorrie and she came from one of the remote suburbs or as we liked to call it, the country. Her clothes were old-fashioned and she wore too much makeup. The most offensive thing she did in the eyes of the other girls was to treat Mrs. Chapman and the other staff members with respect. Dorrie arrived at the facility in a nervous and highly unstable condition. You could see the fear increase in her eyes each day as she was pushed and prodded by even the younger residents. They stole or destroyed her meager clothing and there was hardly a day she was not brought to tears by some act of hatred. I observed Dorrie's struggle without sympathy. Whenever a trickle of compassion tried to emerge from the new me, I quickly pushed it to the back of mind by telling myself it was not any of my business. After all, I had my own objectives to protect. It seemed that with the academic successes I'd achieved that I was well on my way to acquiring exactly what I wanted and deserved.

During the spring of the following year, I was in chemistry class when one of the hall monitors came to retrieve me from the classroom. I reported to the counselor's office with slide rule still in hand to be told,

"We're so sorry but we just received a phone call notifying us that your mother has died."

I was speechless. Before I realized what I was doing, I threw the slide rule into a wall to the side of the teacher's desk. Tears began to roll down my cheeks and I was so shaken that the teacher had to call for an assistant to help her ease me into a chair. I had managed to avoid crying in the presence of other people since my hearing months ago at Juvenile Court. The only time I permitted myself the luxury of crying was on the long ride to East Liberty while I sat alone in the back of the bus. In my heart and mind I had been fighting a battle to survive on my own terms. These few words spoken by my counselor had turned a sunny beautiful day full of hope into absolutely the worst day of my life.

How could she leave me? I didn't want to live with her because she was sick, not because I didn't love her. Had I done anything to disappoint her? The questions and self-doubt began to engulf me while I sat in the counselor's office.

Over the following days that led to the funeral, I returned in a cloud of grief to the Village. My father was by then very emaciated by the ruthless bone cancer that he'd endured. He had probably willed himself to stay alive as long as he continued to receive love and support from my mother. We sat together silently. I could see in his eyes that he was completely lost. I wasn't able to comfort him because I couldn't find the strength to put together more than a few words to anyone.

The prodigal daughter had arranged a sparse service that was held at the funeral home. I approached the casket and touched my mother's hand that had always been warm and nourishing just to encounter an icy cold appendage that was inflexible and in no way even resembled the smooth hand that had lead me through the streets of Pittsburgh.

"I'm sorry Momma. I will be a good girl." I said these words in a whisper despite the choking pain in my throat. The entire day I had repressed a powerful desire to scream. Because of the overwhelming grief, for the first time in my life, I understood why the faithful in the church whale and moan.

As a final insult the prodigal daughter had arranged for our mother to be buried on a muddy, deserted section of the cemetery. I was so outraged and filled with hatred that I had to be restrained from attacking her by one of my cousins.

I never saw my father alive again. Immediately after the funeral, he had been institutionalized by the prodigal daughter. His brave bout with cancer lasted for almost six years. He succumbed shortly after my mother died. His last few hours were spent telling the nursing staff that he was happy because my mother was standing at the foot of his bed waiting to take him home.

With the help of some greedy cousins, the prodigal daughter managed to strip anything of value from the property in the gully. The crooked house and land were finally lost to the county. She did not bother to pay the taxes. It was common knowledge in the Village that she managed to convert to scotch or bourbon every dime of the modest profit from the sale of my parent's personal possessions.

Word of her behavior reached me because some of the girls at the home attended my church. Absolutely nothing could make me feel better. Not the trips to East Liberty, not the challenge to achieve success. Slowly, I began to be filled with an intense resentment and anger that threatened to drag me down a path I never thought it was possible to travel.

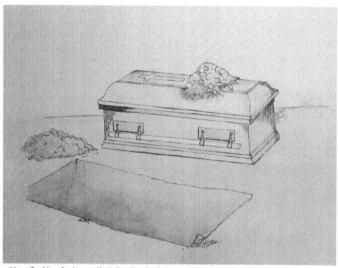

"As a final insult, the prodigal daughter had arranged for our mother to be buried on a muddy, deserted section of the cemetery." Illustrated by Holly N. Avery 2012.

CHAPTER 32 -- MISPLACED HATRED

Dorrie was assigned to Allegheny and there she and I barely crossed paths. I didn't want anyone to know I lived in Termon Avenue Home. Her presence at my school became a threat to my image. I avoided riding the bus to school with her and grew to silently resent her existence in my domain.

Perhaps Mrs. Chapman noticed a negative change in my behavior. She seemed to be more determined than ever to talk to me. The increased summons to her office only further antagonized me.

"You've never been disrespectful, but I don't really know what to write in your file to show your counselor you're ready to go out on your own." This was her way of beginning every encounter.

I sat in the chair and didn't try to hide my impatience with the redundant conversation. "I will go to college after high school, Mrs. Chapman. Now may I be dismissed?"

A long month had gone by since the death of my mother, but she had never breeched the subject. While reaching into a bag of potato chips on the side of her desk she said, "Your mother would be happy if you would be more open with us."

I glared at her because we both knew she barely had spoken to my mother during the entire time I had been at the home. "May I be dismissed?" I was now completely full of hatred for the manner in which she was trying to manipulate me. Perhaps this confrontation served to remove any inhibitions I had to manifest the sense of fear and anxiety that was literally tearing me apart inside.

"Well, alright. You girls have got to learn that we are here to help you." Mrs. Chapman's keys rattled as she opened the door of her office to let me out.
The next day I went to school still consumed by anger. After lunch, I encountered Dorrie in the bathroom and patiently waited for all the other girls to leave us alone before confronting her in front of the mirror. She was putting on another layer of the cheap makeup that she so dearly loved when she realized that I was standing beside her.

"You bitch! You think you're so much better than everyone else. Kissing Mrs. Chapman's ass and everything! You don't belong here!" I moved closer and closer to her and snatched the lipstick from her hand. "Here, I'll show you how to wear this shit." I said as I snatched the tube from her hand and began to smear it all over her face.

"Please, don't hurt me." She begged in a low pitiful voice while her tears began to cause the cheap eye makeup to run down her face. "Please, tell me what you want. I'm sorry, I'm sorry!" I showed no mercy as I grabbed her hair and pushed her face into the mirror.

I never answered or even thought about her questions. Instead, I began to drag her into one of the stalls where I bent her over the toilet and quickly pushed her head into the bowl. She never screamed but only continued to beg and moan. At some point, I released her, and she crumbled to the floor. As I towered over her, I repeatedly dared her to tell anyone what had happened. "Keep your damn mouth shut, bitch!" I kicked her in the side and pushed her face without much resistance into the slippery bathroom floor.

I heard her softly continue to cry as I dried my hands. Dorrie and I didn't have one class together. I knew I would not have to encounter her until later that afternoon at the home. The only fear I had was that she would tell a school official. This never happened. I boarded the bus for the return trip home that afternoon without even a remote feeling of remorse.

When I arrived on the grounds of the institution, I was surprised to find it full of what seemed to be the entire population of the facility. One of the younger girls ran up to me and said, "We always knew that Dorrie was crazy." Someone else added, "Yep, and look now what she's doing. Threatening to commit suicide? Who cares?"

"What? Suicide? Why?" I asked these questions but already knew the answers.

"Who knows. She's screwed up anyway." They answered.

"Where is she now?" I threw my books on the front porch because I knew exactly why Dorrie had suddenly cracked.

"Mrs. Chapman called the police. They said she headed for the boulevard. Going that way..." They pointed in the direction of downtown.

I started to run towards the four lane highway. I didn't know what I would do once I found her, but I realized I had to try. The cars darted by and my regret increased with each step.

Suddenly, I saw Dorrie standing in the middle of the McKees Rocks Bridge. Beneath the bridge laced the dark waters of the Ohio River. She was poised to jump. I knew I had driven her to this point. I continued to run until I was about 50 feet away from her on the bridge. Ironically, this was the same side of her that I had been on earlier that day when I pushed her face into the mirror.

"Dorrie, I'm sorry! Please, what are you doing? Don't. My God what can I say! Please Dorrie, I am so sorry!" I begged her over and over again and she stood there motionless without answering while the strong wind from the river seemed determined to tear her from the edge of the bridge.

"Come on over the rail, please. I apologize. Oh please, don't do this." She was holding on by only one hand and I knew I didn't have the strength to grab her to save her.

By now, the police had found us. An officer pushed me aside and began to talk to Dorrie. "Ok, ah, Dorrie. Dorrie we're here to help you."

I was by then sobbing uncontrollably. It appeared Dorrie was well prepared to take her own life, and I had surely caused the entire thing. After almost an hour, she was rescued. Unfortunately, I now added a deep sense of shame to the preexisting feelings of hatred and resentment I insisted on carrying around without the benefit of sharing with any other human being.

Dorrie was either not permitted or unable to return to the home. I never found out exactly what happened to her. Everyday, I expected Mrs. Chapman to suddenly appear with the paddle in her hand to thrash the daylights out of me. It is fair to assume that Dorrie never told anyone about my twisted behavior. I would have done anything to prevent the truth coming to light about the part I played in her breakdown. This fear kept me from inquiring about her disappearance. The fact that I managed to avoid even a chastisement by Mrs. Chapman didn't help me feel justified or give me the nerve to confess. I kept my mouth shut and resigned myself to carry this one to my grave.

CHAPTER 33 -- VIOLENCE AND INSPIRED HOPE

After the Dorrie incident, I became almost obsessed in my determination to focus on the college entrance exams and leave Pittsburgh. I no longer knew which objective was most important. Everyday, I began to wonder whether or not I was even a decent person. Connections that had supported and provided guidance to me were either dead or inaccessible. In an effort to start a clean and unencumbered life, I had decided after the death of my mother to also avoid contact with the Village. I was too confused to be depressed and unwilling to talk to anyone about anything. Now when I cried on the way to East Liberty I wept because in my heart I hoped that my real mother would miraculously appear and take me away from a life that had become empty and full of grief.

Meals in the dining hall even began to take on an ominous tone. Ora suddenly seemed to be switching her attention in my direction. I looked up from my plate, because I felt as if someone was watching me, the first time I noticed Ora's threatening behavior.

Unfortunately, I was right. Her beady eyes remained fixed on me so intently that I knew I was in trouble. This was the way she always began to torment and stalk an enemy.

She was now only a few months away from being released from the home. A rumor was circulating that she would be institutionalized in a secure facility. I had been in the home for months and knew Ora was prone to switch targets for her fits of anger. The first time she locked a cruel stare in my direction I was able to avoid looking her directly in the eye. This was my only defense against her. I was positive that this alone would discourage her. Eventually, she turned her head away from me. After some consideration I convinced myself that perhaps I had been mistaken about her intentions. Unfortunately, over the next two weeks her focus repeatedly returned to me over the dinner table. Now there was no doubt that I was indeed the new target of Ora's frustrations.

One Saturday afternoon after I had done my chores, I went back to my second floor dormitory to grab a light jacket before leaving for East Liberty. As I entered the room, I observed Ora sitting on her bed. Once again I successfully avoided eye contact. After getting the jacket from my small closet I went through the door again and started to descend the slick wooden stairs. Suddenly, I felt a sharp blow on the top of my head. I grabbed the banister because the entire room had started to turn. At that moment I actually saw lights flash in front of my eyes.

"That's it, you yellow bitch!" I heard Ora's voice behind me and realized that the only reason I hadn't fallen face first down the steps was because she was holding me around the neck. "I know what your sorry ass did to Dorrie!" Once again she hit me with some object that this time landed on the side of my face. She shook me violently like a rag doll and began to rant and rave at the top of her voice. "She was my friend and you hurt her! Didn't you?"

The only thing I could do was cover my face and hope she didn't break my teeth. She was a massive and muscular woman who towered over me by at least six inches and out weighed me by perhaps as much as fifty pounds. I couldn't respond to her because the hold around my neck was strangling me.

I must have collapsed because the next thing I knew I woke up to see her on top of me at the bottom of the steps. "I'm gonna kill you, cow!" There were now people trying desperately to pull her off me.

There was no doubt that Ora had tried to kill me. The whole thing did not make sense. I was an honor student well on my way to college who had suddenly received a strong dose of retribution and survived. Somehow, the blows to my head with a piece of wood didn't fracture my skull and the cuts and bruises slowly healed. For weeks I was in pain, but I refused to complain because I knew that I deserved the punishment.

The beating at Ora's hands did result in a change of attitude by my fellow inmates. Instead of ignoring me, now some of them tried to hold conversations. One day one of the residents of the treasured third floor advised me that she had a friend that wanted to meet me. He was described as outgoing, intelligent and handsome. I agreed to meet him. The next weekend he came to call during regular visitation hours.

His name was Albert Anthony and he lived in my favorite side of town, East Liberty near the university. The most important thing that he brought back into my life was laughter. We began to date, and I often went to his high school to see him play basketball. Albert absolutely knew everybody. He was also as fond as I was of riding the bus all over Pittsburgh. We attended dances, and for the first time in years I again had a real friend.

The one thing that Albert wanted to know more about was always me. He asked questions about my mother, the Village, my old high school and encouraged me to keep focusing on my objective to attend college. I walked through the dangerous streets of Pittsburgh with him and learned first hand how to survive. We were the same age but he was much wiser. Through Albert I began to learn to trust people again. He never asked me for anything I didn't want to give him and exercised a great deal of patience.

From the beginning, I was strongly attracted to Albert. His clothes were always neatly pressed and he wore a three-quarter length leather coat and a cool hat that he kept tilted just so on his head. He taught me that French kissing was an art and I sat for hours in dark movie theaters in his arms being driven to the point of screaming as he softly stroked my breasts. We planned our times together carefully. Yet, once again I escaped culminating the act with him simply because we never had enough money to afford a hotel room.

Due to Albert's entrance into my life and his encouragement, I began to see myself as a person of worth. He insisted that our world be only all about me and I was content. Albert assured me repeatedly that all he wanted to do was to make me happy. We dated every weekend and sometimes he would drop by my school at the end of the day. Most evenings we talked to each other for almost an hour over the phone. I truly believed that I now had someone that I could rely on without question. He had to always call me because the only telephone available to me to receive calls at the home was a pay phone. Nothing seemed impossible when I was around him.

The SAT exam was scheduled for a Saturday morning. During the week preceding the exam, I focused on gymnastics practice, band practice and exam preparation. Albert called regularly to inquire if I needed anything. I assured him I was ready. Thursday afternoon I went to gymnastics practice and during an attempt to dismount the balance beam I misplaced my base hand and landed in the lower small of my back on the beam that was about four feet off the floor.

The spotters rushed to my assistance and I tried to lift myself off the mat. The teacher advised me to lay still and applied a cold compress. I could barely walk to the bus stop. Somehow, I managed to make my way back to the home. That evening when Albert called I couldn't get out of bed. I was in so much pain that I missed school on Friday. That evening I still couldn't walk from my bed to the bathroom without help.

Albert called again around eleven in the late evening on Friday. By this time, I was able to slowly struggle down the stairs to take his call. "What if you have to miss the test Baby? Can't you take it again later this year?" The concern was obvious in his voice. I was touched by his compassion and I realized that he was very worried.

"I'm going to take the test. I can't miss this opportunity because it's the last time it's given this year. I'll have to wait until next year and not be accepted into some of the colleges with my class. I just can't screw this up." I kept assuring him I felt better. No matter what I said he didn't seem to be convinced.

The next day the rain started to fall very early in the morning. I struggled to dress and carefully made my way down the stairs. Breakfast was out of the question. I was afraid to sit down. I didn't want to take the chance that I couldn't get back up. I walked the quarter mile to the bus stop. The pain continued to race through my lower back and down my left leg. Somehow, I managed to take and pass the exam with a moderate score. I don't remember anything about the ride home except the relentless pain.

Albert indicated that he was proud of me while telling me that he was sure now that I was crazy in the same breath. He came by the home later that evening. After watching me hobble down the stairs, he accused me of trying to showboat. "Leave it to you to make a tough thing even harder." With this said he took me by the hand and helped me down the last two steps. I didn't know why he cared so much about me, but I was sure what we had was the real thing. That night for the first time Albert told me he loved me.

We continued to date and grow together into better people. Mrs. Chapman even seemed to like him. One day during the middle of my senior year, Albert failed for the first time to pick me up at the home for our usual Saturday evening date. Mrs. Chapman noticed me sitting on the front porch waiting for him and asked, "So, where is your young man?"

"I'm sure he'll show up soon." I answered while continuing to look down the road hoping to see Albert turn into the driveway. He had to transfer twice on the bus to get to the home. I didn't want to admit to Mrs. Chapman that I hadn't received my usual evening phone call last night.

"Hey Baby. Look I'm sorry I've just been busy, that's all." This was the only explanation that he offered when he finally called a few weeks later. His voice sounded a bit strange but he assured me that he wasn't sick or in trouble.

"Have I done something? Are you ok?" I didn't want to be too pushy, but after so much time between phone calls I was more than a little concerned. We didn't have any mutual friends. I had never met his mother or baby brother that he sometimes mentioned. Albert told me that he had plans for the future, but this experience had shown me that I really didn't know as much about him as he did about me. The only way I had to reach him was the one phone number he gave me which he advised me was his home phone number. I had tried to call him but each time no one answered.

"Sure, I'm just fine. Are you making any progress with the admission applications?" As usual he immediately turned the conversation into one that focused on me.

We talked about specific colleges for a short period of time. When I again tried to ask anything about his situation he immediately changed the subject. The conversation came to an abrupt end when he suddenly told me that he had to go take care of some business and he would call again later. He did not call that night or for many nights to follow.

Some months later, one of Albert's cousins started to date one of the girls at the home. I found out from him that Albert's had been hospitalized with tuberculosis. He also warned me that I should be tested as soon as possible. I took the health department's skin test and the results were negative. For months, every night I continued to wait for his phone call by the foot of the stairs.

CHAPTER 34 -- WHITE CONFUSION

A month prior to my graduation, I suddenly started to wonder about the Village. I was now more aware of the positive changes that were being made in the inner city. My senior year at Allegheny found me completely detached from this small section of Pittsburgh. I arranged with my Aunt Gert to return for a short visit. I hoped to somehow reconnect to this place and the people that had been such a major influence in my life. Above all, I wanted to see if anything had changed.

I remembered the bitter facts. It was easy to recall that both young and old male members of the Village seemed to require especially careful scrutiny. Basically, the community view appeared to be that Village males should only be allowed to assume one of only two menial positions of janitor and night watchman at the neighborhood stores. It was made clear by the absence of local job possibilities that an ambitious Village male had only one option. The first step towards financial independence required a trip to the other side of town by trolley. Once there, an application could be completed for one of the high paying jobs in one of the bustling, steel mills that surrounded Pittsburgh.

Females of the Village were offered more prestige and exposure to the workings of the individual family structures of the neighborhood. They brought to their jobs superior cooking and cleaning skills from a childhood spent performing thankless labor in the deep South. Often, the white employers soon modified and integrated their housekeeping methods and personal tastes into that of the lives of their employees. An excellent example can be illustrated by stating that holiday meals in the Village were often augmented by the inclusion in the menu of items like authentic German potato salad, festive Italian cold cuts and pungent Scandinavian cheeses.

My mother had been employed by a rich German immigrant. He was also a tight fisted professional who seemed to enjoy the mysterious work that he did in one of the many office buildings downtown. His relentless quest to pay attention to the smallest of details demanded the house be cleaned exactly according to his precise guidelines. As per instruction, she washed clothes by hand and hung them on the line at a certain time of the afternoon when the sun was just in the right position. Everything that was cloth in the house required ironing and had to adhere to an exact folding pattern. The massive silver collection was a day's chore to maintain and polish. A normal workday for her began at seven in the morning and she rarely was able to return home earlier than six that evening.

A side benefit to my mother's employment was that we got all the rich German's hand-me-downs. This included canned goods that no longer held his interest, linen less than a few months old which he labeled too worn for any good use and exotic leftovers from his many parties. The rich German did respect my mother's hard work ethic. He repeatedly admitted to her that good help was extremely hard to find. She infrequently asked for time off and would even go to work when her blood pressure soared out of control. It was not uncommon for him to send food and often cash to our home during the few times she did find it necessary to miss work. When his contribution arrived she did not seem to view it as an act of kindness because she usually said, "He's just too lazy to go out and find someone else that'll work like a dog."

Post World War II feelings still ran very deep and absolutely defied common sense. The Jews in the neighborhood did not become the beloved people of the overall community despite the Holocaust. In school the eating of kosher food and holiday exceptions to the normal academic schedule only served to set them further apart. Their determination to support and protect one another and their uncanny ability to earn and control money was viewed with envy. Members of the neighborhood had to let them buy property wherever they wanted and this grew to be an irritating and unsettling situation. Jews owned businesses and always seemed to be in total support of each other. The Jewish children were content in their religion and unconcerned or threatened by the resentment of their white peers.

Italian members of the neighborhood banded together. In the work place they continued to speak their native language. The assumption regarding working for an Italian eatery was that an English-only speaker may not be welcome. Respect was given to them because of their culinary skills and passionate nature. This colorful group found themselves in the middle of the white-only hierarchy. The homes of this segment of the neighborhood were easy to identify by applying basic olfactory senses to detect a common generous use of exotic spices and garlic. For the most part, they were not financially capable of occupying the larger and more elaborate houses. Instead, they usually found themselves in often cheap frame constructions with very small front yards that were less than fifteen feet from their next door neighbor who could easily be a Polish family.

It was almost a curse to be Polish. In many ways their lives paralleled those of the Village members. Their last names frequently ended in "ski" which made it very easy to separate them from their German and Italian white brothers. At some point the label of stupid began to relentlessly be applied to describe people of Polish ancestry. The Polish parents frowned on the use of their native language by their children. Perhaps they felt that this would prove their ability to assimilate. The jobs they were offered paid little and their culinary abilities centered on the preparation of hardy bland tasting foods that offered little popular appeal.

The pompous German children frequently tried to dominate their emotional and proud Italian and supposedly dumb Polish brothers. The ridiculous conflict polluted everything including even elementary school spelling bees. High school nomination processes for prestigious awards like the national merit scholarship did not escape the white inter-racial hatred. A positive result of having observed the ceaseless "white-on-white" bickering did result. We, the children of color, began to doubt that it was a great idea to be part of a world ruled by only white people who constantly fought amongst themselves for superiority.

At this time, in the national community, the fight for equal rights and integration dominated the attention and actions of most of America. In all states in the union there was some sort of attempt to move towards equality. Since the prevailing attitude in the neighborhood was that they didn't have a problem with the Negroes, the need to make changes was not realized. Politicians all over the metropolitan area continued to declare that Pittsburgh as a whole had made strides long ago to successfully combat prejudice. The possible existence of a Negro problem brought defensive statements from them such as: "They already have access to an equal and free education," "They never were required to sit at the back of the bus," and "They hold jobs with a union card and work alongside white men in the mills." These premises were used by the neighborhood to dispute the need for even one small behavioral modification on their part.

By now, inter-racial friendships existed and were mildly tolerated. But, they did not endure. The integrated scouting organizations continued to encourage the community to work together. It was not uncommon for a weekly meeting to be held in the home of a neighborhood supporter. Conversely, the Village still did not host integrated functions. Any event that was designed as a common endeavor would always take place in their neighborhood.

Inter-racial dating could cause an extreme reaction from both sides of the divisive bush. Several of us tried to establish after-school contacts with our neighborhood peers. I once stood beside the hedge outside the home of one girl in the neighborhood for over an hour hoping that she would see me and invite me into her home. The boys of the Village took on the challenge of inter-racial dating. Wisely, they did not attempt this until a few years after the death of President Kennedy.

Finally, a common denominator was thrust upon the neighborhood and the Village that caused everyone to form a united front. An irrational war started and dragged on as it robbed both sides of the lives of their sons. The young men had played together on football fields to the cheers of the Village and the neighborhood. Hope for the future had already been placed in their hands. Vietnam more than anything before it made both sides stop and prioritize.

Hardly a family was untouched by the disgraceful exhibit of imperialism abroad. Some with heavy hearts attended funerals and others were grateful to have their battered sons come home. The blessing often turned to chaos. The next three decades the former soldiers battled nightmares. The community was unequipped to deal with the after effects of agent orange symptoms and drug abuse. A pressing reality closed in and brought with it a sick post-war recessionary economy. My generation was stumbling because of the premature absence of some of its very best members.

Even the most determined segregationist became aware that a remedy was not possible if it was based on the needs of only one segment of society. It was a time that demanded unprejudiced solutions. The Village members did not have much faith that a substantial change could occur. After all, the controllers of the purse-strings were exclusively white. Speeches made by one or the other white elected official passionately promised economic relief. They said that they recognized a need for a united front to provide solutions for the entire community. In practice, their actions revealed that they still held close the idea that if they did too much for the Village they would no longer appear to be in control.

Barriers that had been constructed to keep separate cultures apart suddenly weren't important. The divisive hedge was slated to be torn down. It was an act of condemnation that left the Village members feeling hollow and tired. The local newspaper coverage claimed that neighborhood members felt extremely proud. Unfortunately, the community seemed to not realize that the rest of the world had progressed beyond praising this type of meager and embarrassing symbolism.

One rainy morning a small crowd gathered to watch the hedge fall to the ground. A sad fact was to be realized shortly after the completion of the ceremony. It was painfully obvious that while the purse string controllers had met to decide the fate of a mere inanimate object, the surviving members of the generation of the children from both sides of the bush had already perished or opted to quietly move away.

CHAPTER 35 -- A DEPARTURE AND A BEGINNING

Senior year, 1966, continued to be full of personal achievements. It seemed that for a while I was on my way to a future full of promise. Albert never really tried to reenter my life during this period. Since I didn't have any way to get in contact with him after a few months, I gradually stopped thinking that every time the phone rang in the hallway it would be him.

Classes progressed well and my grade point average remained high. The next step was to meet with my counselor to discuss my options. We had been coached by our English Literature teacher as to what questions to ask and how to complete the admission applications. I felt prepared and thanks to Albert I had a sense of confidence and now felt emotionally strong enough to compete for a good scholarship or grant.

The counselor was an elderly white woman who mostly seemed content to stay the entire day in her office. She was known to fight for the students to be admitted to only the best colleges. My white fellow students at the same academic level were already talking about admission to Penn State, Wellesley, and even Princeton. I tried to keep an open mind. I really didn't know much about what college or university would be best suited for my needs. At this time, I still lacked a clear idea as what to declare as a major. Therefore, I was open to any suggestion about an undergraduate school. I had worked hard and I was sure I deserved the best opportunity.

Encouragement was offered by my teachers who felt I had excellent potential. I had done a good job in their opinion as the moderator for the senior play, *Our Town*. Besides this achievement they all seemed to agree that I should attend a school that offered an academic challenge because I seemed to flourish under pressure. That year leading up to the meeting with the counselor, I made it a point to speak individually to all my teachers. I didn't want to make a mistake in my choice of colleges.

The day arrived for me to meet with the counselor and I eagerly knocked on her door. "Come in and sit over there." She said this while motioning towards a seat to the left of her desk. "Now, let's take a look at that record. Yes, you transferred here as a sophomore late in the school year and, it seems you've done pretty well here. Always tested high on aptitude tests and kept your grades up. No misbehavior and few days missed." She continued to read the record in silence at this point.

After a few minutes she looked up and after closing the folder sat back in her chair. "Do you have any plans?"

"No ma'am. I have been to the library and read about a few colleges, but I really wanted to talk to you before going any further. I've never really been out of Pittsburgh. I just want to go to a school that will challenge me." I was basically repeating what I had been told by my teachers at this point.

"But you don't know what you want to major in, right?" She asked while beginning to lean forward in her chair.

"I have interests in many subjects. So, I think I should major in Liberal Arts. Do I have to know what I want to major in to get started?" I decided to press her for answers rather than sit there and wait for her to tell me what to do.

"It would be advisable, if you want to go to one of the better schools. Also, if you don't know what you want I probably can't get you financial aid to these schools either. Will you have parental help? No, wait, I'm sorry your parents are deceased, right?" She took advantage of the pause and stood up in front of her window.

"Yes ma'am. I'm on my own. But I've always wanted to go to college. I know I can do the work. Maybe they'll let me work on campus or something. I think they call it work study. All I've ever wanted to do was go to college." Suddenly, I realized I was begging this woman for an opportunity. I was confused because I thought before I came into her office that I had already proven myself.

"I may have something for you. There's a new program by a group called the United Negro College Fund that offers scholarships to qualified students to schools that are mostly in the South. I have a catalog here, somewhere." She went to her file cabinet and pulled out a brochure. "Here, take this home and read about it. Some people need to be with their own and this might be the best thing for you."

I took the pamphlet and looked at her hoping to hear her mention one of the schools that I really knew I now wanted to attend. Obviously, she didn't think I had what it takes to make it at Penn State, Carnegie or any other school besides those that were all black. She motioned for me to get up because as far as she was concerned the meeting was over. "Let me know which colleges you apply to so that I can indicate it in your permanent record."

"Yes ma'am." I rose from the chair, left her office and walked to the gymnasium where I sat on the bleachers and stared at the UNCF information. Maybe she was right. Perhaps my permanent record indicated that I was actually slow. After all, I thought, she is the authority.

I applied to five of the UNCF colleges and was accepted at all of them with generous offers for full or partial scholarships or grants. In order to get started without any clothes or even a suitcase, I had to obtain a student loan from Mellon Bank. Fortunately, I also received support in the form of cash and clothing from a distant cousin on my mother's side of the family. I wasn't shocked by what happened when I dropped by the counselors office to update her on my progress. She barely acknowledged my presence even after I had patiently waited to see her for almost an hour. The conversation was brief. She quickly dismissed me by asking only one question. "Which college will you attend?" This was the extent of her interest and support.

The weekend before prom night I packed my new luggage and recently acquired clothing. It was necessary for me to miss graduation and the prom in order to report to Bishop College in Dallas, Texas for early admissions. Saturday morning I decided I should return to the Village.

I rode the bus to the familiar stop in the neighborhood and spent the first two hours drifting up and down the streets of my childhood. The revolution now seemed silly as I sat on the curb in front of where I had placed the pop bottle that infamous night. Each home that I had loved so much and craved to be inside in the exclusive neighborhood looked basically the same. Above all, I was certain that I would still be considered by the residents to be an unwelcome guest.

Some of the older adults of the Village were still alive at that time. They were especially happy to see me and even happier to know that I was headed off to college. They each hugged me and wished me well. One neighbor called me aside and said, "You know me and your mama were close friends? Well, I always told her she was too hard on you and that you were a good girl. I don't think she ever got over comparing you to your sister." Her kind words instantly liberated me completely from any feelings of insecurity or doubt that I still harbored towards my mother. Prior to receiving this information, I honestly believed that I had successfully dealt with my mother's death. Now, I realized that I still harbored the irrational fear that there was something horrible that I had done which had somehow contributed to her demise.

I went back to Sam's house and received a bear hug from his mother along with the traditional cookie. Cookies at her house always tasted special. Sam was by now a sophomore at Pitt. I found Aunt Gert on her front porch and I sat with her for a while answering a thousand questions about where I was going and what I'd be doing. She told me that Jerry and his wife from the horde had just had a beautiful baby. As the evening moved on it was obvious that she was still in the habit of waiting for my uncle to come home. I left the Village at nearly nine o'clock and he was still missing in action.

Sunday morning, before going to the Greyhound Bus Terminal downtown, I met with Mrs. Chapman for the last time. I didn't tell her that I would not be back. I think she knew I wouldn't return. At the end of our session she simply said, "Well, do well out there in Texas." She picked up her keys and opened the door for me. We stood in silence on the front porch while I waited for a taxicab.

I was an inexperienced traveler, but I knew it was important to arrive early at the terminal. I wanted to try to at least appear to be as relaxed as possible. All the horror stories I'd heard about panhandlers and terminal pickpockets were running around in my head. The terminal was full of faces that I had never seen. I wanted familiarity but I was dizzy and elated to find diversity. The ticket agent gave me a formal boarding pass, and I checked in a trunk and three suitcases. I took advantage of the extra time and went outside in order to get one last look towards the downtown area. I recalled walking every street at the side of my mother while she wheeled, 'dealed' and balanced her many credit accounts. I tried to breath deeply in order to smell the fish sandwiches we both loved on Market Street near the Farmer's Market.

It wasn't long before I heard the announcement, "Bus departing slot 15 for St. Louis, Dallas and all points West."

I found the gate quickly. After standing in line for only a short while, I gave the driver my ticket at the door of the bus and then went down the aisle to a seat near the window. I was filled with joy and the fear of strangers was soon replaced by a sense of comfort. I knew that many people had given up a great deal and worked hard to help me arrive at this day. As the dramatic skyline of Pittsburgh disappeared behind the entrance to the Washington Tunnel, I felt empowered and blessed by their sacrifices. The diversity of the neighborhood and the warmth of the Village would always be a part of me.

For the first time in my life, I was content to be in my own skin. I couldn't help smiling deeply as I shut my eyes in an attempt to hold back the tears of joy and liberation.

Illustrated by Holly N. Avery 2012.

EPILOGUE

At first, like many writers, I felt it was important to document a time and place that has now changed in so many ways that it is beyond recognition. I also believed that even the survival of an unknown baby-boomer merited being told. The vast majority of us have lead common lives when compared to our celebrity peers with their Academy Awards, Nobel Prizes or Rhodes Scholarships. We've struggled on mostly in obscurity, known only as the targeted audience of self-help books and countless autobiographical works. Yet, we are the survivors and the ceiling breakers that made an impression and a way clear for our children to accomplish more than we ever hoped to achieve.

The era brought to life in this memoir justifies being thoroughly documented and examined. The work is my small contribution to historians that will hopefully explain one day exactly what our generation contributed to society. The entire project succeeded mostly because of the patience and generosity of encouraging friends. I frankly wanted to quit many times and for many reasons - all of which at the time seemed to perfectly validate saving the file for a final time and shutting off the computer. They repeatedly volunteered to read the manuscript, correct my tendency to run on sentences and enthusiastically critiqued the entire work without complaint. It is for them, and you the reader, that I write what they recommended, an epilogue to the story for the purpose of clarification.

I wish I could recant a Hollywood ending full of personal acclaim and success after leaving Pittsburgh. Unfortunately, my birth parents remained a total mystery until well after my thirtieth birthday. My flesh and blood sister found me living in Tennessee with my first child and

Vietnam damaged first husband. By this time, I had foolishly dropped out of college before my senior year for reasons of love and passion.

The reunion with my biological mother was emotional and eventful. Like so many things it seemed to prosper for a few years just to fail miserably in the end. She harbored a strange and unforgiving hatred for her siblings. In addition to this, she refused to share any personal knowledge about my real father and selfishly took this valuable information to her grave. In the end, I did learn one lesson from her: How to suck the very life out of a secret. For this reason, I'm trying harder than ever to not be anything like my real mother.

My Mom used to like to say, "Thank God, and if the creek don't rise." She said this when she was relieved about something and felt things were definitely headed in the right direction. I'm now a doctoral student at a prominent university trying to finally finish one of the degrees my mother in the Village desperately wanted me to acquire so many years ago. I still crave her approval, and I honestly believe that at this point in my life she would certainly be proud.

Afterword

How in the world did Linda Hall turn out to be such a strong, dynamic, accomplished woman? Did the never-ending tasks she performed as a child give her the tenacity to continue to pursue numerous degrees under challenging circumstances? Did feelings of isolation and abandonment lead her to have a heart for people of diverse backgrounds and cultures? Who were the people in the Village that had the most influence on her life? What impact did her childhood experiences have on the kind of wife and mother she became? What happened to her between the time she left Pittsburgh and ended up in California? These are just a few questions I have about the book's author.

I had no idea what happened to Linda after she left the small town where we spent our childhood. During the years we lived in the "Village," I recall her constantly spouting Spanish as we walked home from the school bus stop or the store. A visit to her house would find her busy bringing water from the spring to boil, or washing clothes in a tin tub with a scrub board. She would practice on her violin for hours until a squeaky noise became a melody. The only thing I remember her complaining about was that her mother often asked why she couldn't be more like the daughter of her friend. Even then, Linda was preparing for her destiny.

It was not until several decades later that Linda and I reconnected in California. After being asked to edit her book, I learned about what she had endured after she was abruptly torn away from the only home and family she had ever known and placed in the Termon Avenue Home. *Three Rivers Crossed* is truly a tribute to the courage and determination of my friend, Linda Jean Hall.

--Savannah Blanchard--

ABOUT THE AUTHOR

Linda Hall is currently a doctoral candidate in Anthropology at the University of California at Santa Barbara where she also attained a BA in Spanish and an MA in Latin American and Iberian Studies. Her graduate research in Ecuador is an examination of how race and ethnicity and sociological theory attempt to explain the contribution of Afro-Ecuadorians to the building of Ecuadorian citizenship. As a member of the Black Diaspora, a wife and mother, Linda continues to construct a meaningful life always based on the values she received during her childhood in the Village.

Made in the USA
Charleston, SC
25 May 2012